kitchen
scraps

PIERRE A. LAMIELLE

kitchen scraps

a humorous illustrated cookbook

whitecap

Whitecap Books is known for its expertise in the cookbook market, and has produced some
of the most innovative and familiar titles found in kitchens across North America. Visit our
website at www.whitecap.ca.

Also visit the Kitchen Scraps website at www.kitchenscraps.ca.

Edited by Grace Yaginuma
Proofread by Paula Ayer
Illustrations by Pierre A. Lamielle
Cover and interior design by Pierre A. Lamielle
Additional typesetting by Setareh Ashrafologhalai, Michelle Mayne, and Mauve Pagé

Printed in China

Library and Archives Canada Cataloguing in Publication

Lamielle, Pierre A.
    Kitchen scraps / Pierre A. Lamielle.

ISBN 978-1-55285-989-6

    1. Cookery. 2. Cookery--Humor. I. Title.

TX714.L347 2009   641.5   C2009-902676-7

The publisher acknowledges the financial support of the Government of Canada through
the Book Publishing Industry Development Program (BPIDP) and the Province of British
Columbia through the Book Publishing Tax Credit.

09 10 11 12 13   5 4 3 2 1

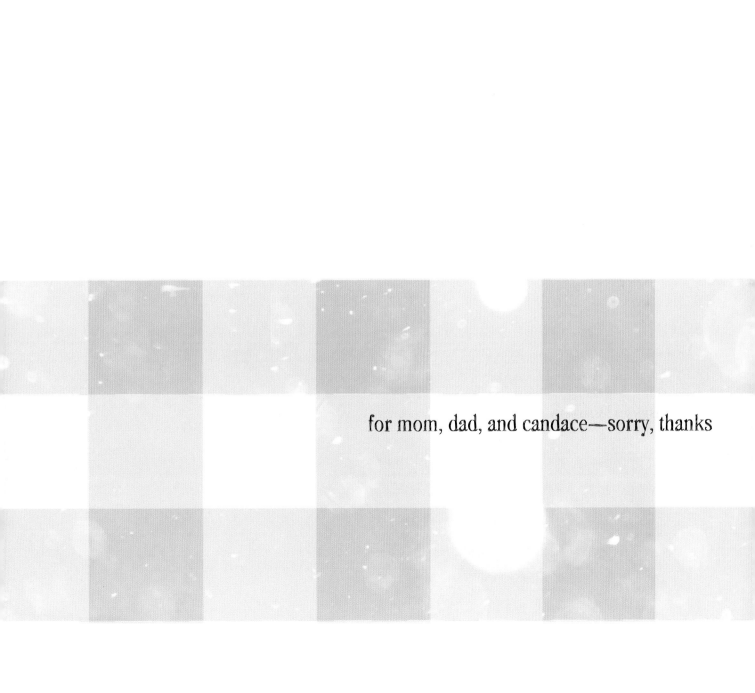

for mom, dad, and candace—sorry, thanks

out of order

This table of contentments is about as helpful as closing your eyes and flipping to a random page.

table of contentments

for lack of a better foreword

What was I thinking, holding out for a superstar celebrity chef to write the foreword to my book? I'm such a moron!

As soon as the first proofs came off the press, I was prancing around like a douche-auteur, showing off the book and sending out review copies by email all willy-nilly. To make matters worse, people started saying things like "nifty!" or "neat-o!" and the praise went straight to my rapidly overinflating ego. These delusions of grandeur made me think that maybe one of my culinary heroes might say, "I want to write your foreword."

So I sent some page samples to Anthony Bourdain (because of his irreverence and prose style), Mario Batali (because of his suave and debonair food-itude), Jamie Oliver (because he is charming and sincere, and I have all his books), and Alton Brown (because he is the food nerd I aspire to be). But they all graciously declined, and I should have been happy that with their busy schedules they took the time to say, "No, but thank you for asking."

It should have shushed my ego to a tolerable volume.

But then the page samples started getting phenomenal feedback from great foodites like Ben Schott (everyone must have a copy of *Schott's Food & Drink Miscellany*),

Dorothy Hamilton (the gracious founder of the French Culinary Institute empire in NYC), Bob Blumer (the Surreal Gourmet and a fellow sideways thinker), and Michael Ruhlman (the world's hardest-working food writer).

So my perception of my own importance got more preposterously overinflated. Pretty soon my mind was conjuring images of my favourite gastro-celebrities going head to head over the right (dare I say privilege) to write the foreword.

Then more epicurean heavyweights would pounce into the fray. Gordon Ramsay (because everything he touches is nothing short of perfection) and Martha Stewart (because hers was my first cookbook and I got mad at people in the '90s who gave her flak . . . look who's laughing now) both jump into the kitchen scrap and it gets really good.

Before anybody can claim the victory prize of writing the *Kitchen Scraps* foreword, I awaken from my reverie—face down in a drool-soaked pile of sketches, alone with my deflating ego and a realistic idea for how to fill the desolate foreword page.

PAL

introduction

Before you put this book back on the overstuffed shelf with all the other thousands of cookbooks, flip to a random page and read through one recipe.

If that recipe doesn't make you a) laugh, b) inspired to cook, or c) hungry for more, then you can go ahead and put the book back on the shelf.

So now that you plan on buying this book or have already bought it, then you should get used to flipping to random pages because *Kitchen Scraps* is out of order. And it's not just out of order with a clear lack of organization, it's also out of order on purpose, irreverently.

It is not a cookbook for busy families, it will not make you a kitchen deity, and it will certainly not make you lose ten pounds. *Kitchen Scraps* will delight, offend, and make you hungry.

It seems like not that long ago food was restricted to being on the plate in front of you, whether you were at home, a restaurant, or a friend's house. But things have changed and now food is everywhere.

And food is in your face even when you're not eating it.

food you eat with a

spoon

Spoons are like little shovels. At certain eating events where
a shovel is inconvenient or not permitted, a spoon makes an
excellent substitute.

Get into a good hunched position close to your bowl or plate, and
using an overhand grip, shovel the food quickly into your mouth.

three bears' oatmeal

Once upon a time there lived three bears. A papa bear, a mama bear, and a baby bear in his mid-twenties who wouldn't move out because everything at home was "just right."

One morning, Baby Bear woke up with a mind-numbing hangover. He staggered downstairs to find his parents eating their usual oatmeal—Papa Bear with a steamy hot slab of pan-seared oatmeal *au jus* and Mama Bear with her yummy-mummy oatmeal. His doting mother then brought him a bowl of hair-of-the-bear hangover oatmeal to help him clear the lingering mind fog.

papa bear's pan-seared oatmeal au jus

When most dads think of oatmeal, they think only of constipation relief. Change your dad's mind with this breakthrough oatmeal recipe for big bear men. It will have him grunting in satisfaction instead of consternation.

2 Tbsp butter

1- to 2-inch slice of oat loaf (see recipe below)

¼ cup raisins

½ cup cinnamon *jus* (see recipe below) or apple juice

GET A SOLID FRYING PAN over medium heat. Get the pan warm and toss in your butter. Just as it melts, lay the oat loaf into the melted butter, and just let it mellow for a while. Don't fuss with it, just let the underside get brown and crispy.

Flip it when it is crispy, and finish browning on the other side. Place it in a shallow bowl and set aside.

Crank the heat all the way up and toss in your raisins. When the pan is really hot, deglaze with the cinnamon *jus* or apple juice and let the liquid reduce by half.

Pour the plumped raisins and sweet *jus* over the pan-seared oatmeal, and serve it hot to your pops.

SERVES 1 PAPA BEAR.

OAT LOAF

Make 3 cups of oatmeal according to package instructions. Pour the final product into a non-stick loaf pan, and chill in the fridge covered in plastic wrap. It will last in the fridge for a week, and you can slice off pieces for breakfast daily. If you can portion out 6 slices, each serving is equal to half a cup of cooked oatmeal.

CINNAMON JUS

Bring 1 cup of water, 2 cups of sugar, and 3 cinnamon sticks to a boil. Reduce the heat and gently simmer for 10 minutes. Remove it from the heat and let it cool down to room temperature. Remove the cinnamon sticks, and transfer the syrup into a bottle using a funnel. It makes about 1 cup, and will keep in the fridge for up to 2 weeks.

mama bear's yummy-mummy oatmeal

Thanks to all the yummy mummies who made us kids eat oatmeal, told us to put on clean undies, and read us bedtime stories . . . we love you. Treat mummies with this easy compote of spiced dried fruit. Maybe that's how they maintain those yummy-mummy figures?

oatmeal for 1 serving

1 cup dried fruit (your choice of apricots, cranberries, apples, prunes, pineapples, etc.)

1 tsp spice mix (your choice of cinnamon, cloves, ground ginger, allspice, etc.)

½ cup cranberry juice

1 Tbsp brown sugar or honey

1 tsp each ground flaxseed and wheat germ

almond or soy milk

MAKE OATMEAL ACCORDING to package instructions.

In a separate small pot, combine the dried fruit, spices, cranberry juice, and brown sugar or honey (even though yummy mummy's already sweet enough). Bring to a medium simmer over medium heat, and cook until it becomes sticky and delicious, about 10 minutes or so. But don't let the fruit turn to mush.

Scoop the oatmeal into a pretty bowl, sprinkle on the flax and wheat germ, and top with a nice scoop of the fruit compote. Pour some almond or soy milk overtop.

SERVES 1 YUMMY MUMMY.

baby bear's hair-of-the-bear oatmeal

Who knows more about oatmeal and boozing than the Scottish? This recipe with whisky is a great way to relieve that hangover so you can start piecing together the events from the night before. It may help to understand why there is a half-naked blond woman in your bed calling you "baby." It's amazing how one night of binge drinking can make things go from *just right* to *just wrong*.

1 cup water
½ cup steel-cut oats
big pinch of salt
Scotch whisky to taste
brown sugar and half-and half
    cream to taste

IT'S SO SIMPLE. Just bring the water to a simmer on high heat, then add the oats and salt and drop the heat to medium. Stir the dickens out of it until it is smooth and cooked, about 15 to 20 minutes. Now add a healthy and resuscitating splash of your favourite Scotch whisky, and serve with some brown sugar and cream.

WILL RESUSCITATE 2 RECOVERING PARTY ANIMALS.

bear butt-kicking granola

When bears wake up from their long winter hibernation, they are grumpy and hungry and become big bully bears. They need to bulk up fast, and that means high-calorie food. When bears think high-calorie food they think hikers packing energy bars, trail mix, and granola. Yes, granola usually has tons of fat, carbs, and sugar (surprised? check the box of any store-bought kind). Carbs are good for energy, but without any protein you will crash faster. This awesome recipe is low fat but just the right amount of calories, with lots of crunchy flavour, vitamins, and protein to make you last.

Dry stuff

2 cups quick-cooking oats

¾ cup whole raw almonds

3 scoops vanilla protein powder

3 Tbsp shredded unsweetened
   coconut

2 Tbsp ground flaxseed

1 Tbsp ground ginger or cinnamon

Wet stuff

¾ cup cranberry, orange, or
   pineapple juice

5 Tbsp honey

Fruit medley

1 cup mixed dried fruit (raisins,
   apricots, apples, cranberries,
   whateva)

PREHEAT THE OVEN to 300°F.

In a big bowl, mix all the dry stuff together, then add the wet stuff, and mix with your hand. Don't freak out because it looks like slop—the liquid will all evaporate during baking. Coat your non-stick cooking tray with non-stick cooking spray, or line it with parchment paper. Plop little globs freely all over the baking sheet. Just let it plop, and don't muck with it—the more you muck with it, the more it will glom together.

Blap it in the oven. Every 20 minutes, take the tray out and, with a spatula, flip the granola while breaking it up into slightly smaller pieces. By the third flip (60 minutes of baking), the pieces should be ever-so-slightly damp and bite-sized. Then blap it back into the oven for the last time, baking for 20 more minutes. Without opening the oven door, turn the oven off, and leave the tray in the oven for 2 hours. Cooling it this way is crucial to get the granola crunchy.

Once it's cooled completely, put the granola in a sealable container, and add your dried-fruit medley. Shake it all up and you've got kickass granola.

Serve it with milk, yogurt, or fresh berries, or straight from the container.

MAKES ABOUT 3 CUPS OF BEAR BUTT-KICKING POWER.

BEAR-FISTED BRAWL

You should never actually take on
a bear in hand-to-paw combat, but
if push comes to shove, make sure
you are with a friend who is either
tougher or slower than you. Always
make enough granola for two.

bread of roses

Treat your princess to a breakfast-in-bread-pudding. Make her dreams come true with a royally luscious make-it-the-day-ahead breakfast, which you can both leisurely enjoy while you lie around and come up with reasons not to get out of bed.

butter

3 cups of slightly dried-out French bread, cut into ½-inch cubes with the crusts trimmed

1 egg

¼ cup milk

¼ cup heavy cream

2 Tbsp sugar

2 tsp rosewater

50 g white chocolate, finely chopped or grated

¼ cup green pistachios (shelled)

red rose petals for garnish

whipped cream for fun

THE DAY AHEAD (OR AT LEAST HALF AN HOUR BEFOREHAND):

Grease up a cake pan or moderately deep baking dish with butter.

Put the cubed French bread into a large bowl. In a separate bowl, combine the egg, milk, cream, sugar, and rosewater, and beat until smooth. Pour this over the bread, sprinkle in the white chocolate, and mix it all thoroughly until the bread is all coated with the goopy liquid. Try not to overmix it so it gets all smooshy. You should have soppy bread *chunks*, not bread *pulp*.

Transfer the mess into the greased baking pan or dish, cover with plastic wrap, and blap it in the refrigerator until you're ready to bake.

TO BAKE THE BREAD PUDDING:

Preheat the oven to 325°F.

Remove the plastic wrap, and blap the bread pudding in the oven for an hour, or until a toothpick inserted in the centre comes out very clean.

Allow to cool for a few minutes before serving your loved one. Or you can put it in the fridge to cool completely. Whether hot or cold, scoop into bowls and serve with the pistachios and rose petals scattered across the top. Whipped cream is always welcome with breakfast in bed . . . and it's good on the bread pudding too.

SERVES 2 RAVENOUS LOVERS.

give whirled peas a chance

It's time to think green. I'm talking about peace, love, and understanding for everyone and everything we share this planet with. We are all peas in the same pod.

So why can't we all agree that green is the new world order? Instead of waiting for a change, take hold of this bold green-initiative soup with sweet peas spiked with rejuvenating mint and lemon juice. Use purified water and cane sugar for the purity factor. This just might be the most utopian soup on the planet.

Give whirled peas a chance.

whirled peas soup

15 mint leaves

1 Tbsp lemon juice or white wine
    vinegar

1 Tbsp olive oil

1 cup water

1 tsp kosher or sea salt

1 tsp sugar, preferably cane sugar

2 cups frozen green peas

organic sour cream to garnish

fresh-cracked pepper

IN A BLENDER, place the mint, lemon juice or vinegar, and olive oil.

In a medium-sized pot, combine the water, salt, and sugar. Bring to a boil, then add the frozen peas. As soon as it returns to a boil, carefully dump the whole lot into a blender.

Remove the little plastic thingy from the lid of the blender, and cover the hole with a tea towel. (This stops it from being airtight, which would cause an ugly kick at the start—although the steam can sometimes get hot on your hand.) Start on low, and build up the speed incrementally to the highest setting, then blend on high for 1 minute.

Strain the soup through a fine-meshed sieve into a vessel with a spout for easy pouring, and serve in shallow bowls immediately. Garnish with a gloop of sour cream and a crack of fresh pepper.

RECIPE SERVES 2. TO SERVE THE WHOLE HUMAN RACE, MULTIPLY RECIPE BY APPROXIMATELY 3,364,108,470.

GLOBAL CHILLING

Frozen peas work very well with this recipe. Since peas are harvested and frozen right away they preserve their sweetness quite nicely. If you want to use fresh peas, they must be *very* fresh! Peas begin to lose their sweetness after only a couple days of being picked.

babushka grannies' battle of the borscht

Throughout time, the hands of babushka grannies have been stained red from the battle of the borscht. The Russians cry for meat. The Ukrainians demand tomatoes. The Americans always scream for sour cream. The global borscht rifts have been growing for a thousand and one years. The one thing that unites all versions is the humble red beet. Open your heart to a world of possibilities and help create a borderless planet of peace and harmony for the great borscht.

STIRRING THE POT

Update your traditional borscht with a variety of fresh veggies, like green cabbage, carrots . . . even cucumber. You can add meat too, like beef, pork, chicken, or any kind of sausage. Canned beans will also work. And add some flava flav with rosemary, caraway seed, fennel seed, juniper berries, or garlic.

RED ALERT

No matter how often I eat beets, I am constantly alarmed the next day to discover that I am urinating blood . . . or so it seems. The dye in beets gives your urine a faint red tint and it may come as a shock if you are not expecting it. You've been warned.

12 slices bacon, chopped

1 red onion, roughly chopped

1 bottle dark beer

5 beets, peeled and cut into
   ½-inch dice

15 lil' fingerling potatoes (or small
   new potatoes)

1 red cabbage, cut into
   1-inch chunks

4 cups beef stock

1 small can (14 oz) diced tomatoes

water as needed

zest and juice of 1 lemon

1 bunch fresh dill, roughly chopped

salt and pepper to taste

2 cups sour cream

GET THE BIGGEST pot you have. At least a 4-quart capacity.

To render the fat from the bacon, put it in the cold pot with a good splash of cold water. Turn up the heat to medium-low. The water will start to draw out the bacon fat, and when the water evaporates the bacon will be crispy with the melted fat in the pot. Remove the bacon with a slotted spoon and put it on some paper towel, reserving it as a garnish for later. Drain all but 2 Tbsp of the fat into an old can, not down the drain.

Sauté the onions in the 2 Tbsp of bacon fat on medium-low heat until they become translucent.

Crank the heat all the way up and add the whole bottle of beer. Beat back the foamy uprising with your wooden spoon, and loosen up all the crunchy stuck-on bacon crusties.

Now just giv'er willy-nilly. Pile in the beets, potatoes, and cabbage. Pour in the beef stock and canned tomatoes, and add water until it covers the top of the veggie pile plus 1 inch. Crank the heat until it boils, give it a quick stir, then reduce the heat to medium-low, cover it, and cook for at least 30 minutes. Stir it every couple of minutes, but don't rough up the potatoes.

Before serving, add the lemon zest and juice, the whack of chopped dill, and salt and pepper to taste.

Slop it in bowls, top with a gloop of sour cream, and garnish with the crispy bacon bits. Grab a slab of bread and butta.

CAN FEED A SMALL ARMY OF 6 LARGE-BONED PEOPLE.

foul-mouthed french

The French are foul-mouthed. They find enormous pleasure in cussing, eating stinky cheese, and smoking like chimneys. But for some reason they have a globally recognized technique for kissing that involves a lot of tasting of the other person's mouth. The ultimate contradiction is that the national soup of France is composed nearly entirely of onions.

stinking french onion soup

1 stale French baguette

5 white or yellow medium-sized
onions, *ciseler* (turn the page
for instructions)

3 Tbsp vegetable oil

2 Tbsp butter

1 Tbsp flour

1 glass of red wine

3 sprigs of thyme

bay leaf

4 cups water

salt and pepper

8 oz Gruyère, grated

TEAR UP THE French bread into 2-inch chunks, and put it in an oven at 200°F. (Don't worry about preheating the oven.) Dry out the bread while you prepare everything else.

Ciseler the onions.

Heat a large pot over medium heat. When it's hot, add the oil and the onions. Now you can chill out and, if you have a TV nearby, put on something French with subtitles while you slowly cook the onions . . . because it's going to take a while—about 30 to 40 minutes.

As the onions cook, they will release moisture. Think of it as forcing the onions to perspire in a sauna and cleaning their smelliness from the inside out. The next thing is the onions will slowly start to turn brown. The sugars deep inside the onions are being released and caramelizing.

PARADOX DECODED

By slowly cooking the onions you replace their harsh sulphurous stench with a much more palatable sweetness. To emphasize this sweetness, this recipe uses only water instead of stock, allowing the onion to stand out.

The success of this dish lies in your ability to walk the thin line between golden brown and burnt-to-*merde*. You need enough colour so the onions give the soup flavour that will carry it without the help of stock. Just as they are beginning to look perfectly browned and the bottom of the pan is covered with crispy brown flavour clingers, it is time to melt in the butter. Mix it in smoothly, then sprinkle on the flour and stir it quickly to avoid lumps. Cook this for about 30 seconds. Then crank up the heat and toss in the red wine to deglaze the pan. The liquid will help release all the clingy bits on the bottom, which translate into flavour.

When it stops smelling like raw booze, toss in the thyme, bay leaf, and water. Bring it to a rapid boil and reduce it by a third, approximately 30 minutes.

While your soup reduces, it's a good time to take the bread out of the oven. Then crank up the broil setting for the final meltdown.

When the soup has reduced, taste it for salt and pepper, and season as needed. It may need lots of both at this point (seasoning it before it reduces may result in something too salty).

Fill up a deep bowl with chunks of dried-out French bread. Scoop in the onion soup to cover, making sure you gets lots of onion and also plenty of broth for the bread to soak up. Cover the whole thing with a big messy handful of cheese, and blap it onto a tray and into the oven. Keep an eye on it until the cheese gets crusty, bubbly, and golden-brown delicious.

Serve it sizzling with a bottle of French red wine.

ciseler

In French cooking, like French kissing, technique is very important. Here is what they teach you on the first day of French cooking school . . . how to *ciseler* an onion. If you are going to learn the ultimate French recipe, you should learn the basic French technique for dicing an onion.

STEP UN

Cut off the pointy top of the onion. Then carefully shave off the root end, making sure you leave the onion attached together at the root end. Peel away the dry outer skin.

STEP DEUX

Cut the onion in half, starting by cutting directly through the middle of the root end.

STEP TROIS

Lay the onion half on its flat side, with your hand securing the root end. Keep your fingertips and thumb tucked away for protection. Use the knife to make vertical cuts that cut almost all the way back to the root, but not quite. The onion should stay attached at the root end.

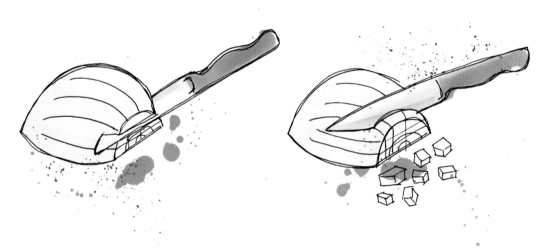

STEP QUATRE

Now carefully make 2 or 3 horizontal cuts most of the way to the back of the onion, but making sure the onion stays attached at the root end.

STEP CINQ

Simply slice the onion from top to bottom, and miraculously and instantly you will have onion *ciseler*.

L'OIGNON QUI ME FAIT PLEURER

After the onion is diced, don't keep hacking it smaller, or it will turn to mushy onion. Mushy onion will make you cry for sure because the juices will make your eyes water. If you manage to *ciseler* carefully and successfully, you won't have to cut the diced onion any smaller, and you won't release all the sad onion juice.

beans and gas
for a cleaner tomorrow

As the world looks toward alternative energy sources, we will have to balance tradition with change. Beans are a good fuel source for us—and require less fuel to produce than beef and cheese. We can all breathe easier knowing we are creating a world with cleaner air . . . well, sort of. Go with the classic baked beans, or "baked wind pills," as they were called back in the pioneer days.

beans and gas

2 cans (19 oz each) mixed beans,
    drained and rinsed

3 Tbsp tomato paste

1 Tbsp dried mustard

1 tsp salt

1 ¼ cups root beer, ginger ale, or
    cola

water as needed

8 slices double-smoked bacon

PREHEAT THE OVEN to 300°F.

Combine all the ingredients except the bacon in an ovenproof dish. Add water if needed . . . the consistency should be soupy, with about an inch of liquid above the beans. Most of the liquid will evaporate or be absorbed by the beans.

Top with the bacon, torn into large pieces. Blap the whole thing uncovered in the oven for 2½ hours. Let it stand for 20 minutes after it comes out of the oven for the sauce to settle.

MAKES ENOUGH FOR 6 TO ENJOY OUTSIDE IN THE FRESH AIR . . . JUST NOT TOO CLOSE TO THE CAMPFIRE.

BEANS, BEANS, THE MUSICAL FRUIT . . .

Beans contain certain carbohydrates that we are not able to break down so easily. They cannot be digested properly in our stomachs and therefore pass through to the lower intestine, where naturally occurring bacteria consume the sugars and create gases, which inevitably have to be expelled. That is the reason why, scientifically speaking . . . the more you eat, the more you toot!

ferocious sheep

High up in the rolling hills of the Himalachians there lives a particularly ferocious herd of sabre-toothed sheep. They graze around the lush green hillsides, eating their fill without fear of being eaten themselves.

With no predators to look out for, their shepherd has it pretty easy. All he ever does is count sheep and sleep . . . He has so much time on his hands and can dedicate long hours to making his favourite shepherd meal.

So what *does* the shepherd of a flock of killer sheep eat?

vegetarian shepherd's pie

Mashed potatoes

5 large russet potatoes, peeled and
    quartered

1 ½ cups sheep's milk (or goat's milk
    or cow's milk), warmed up

6 Tbsp cold butter

salt

Shepherd's pie

2 lb mixed mushrooms, like button,
    cremini, or portobello

1 bottle of beer

5 Tbsp miso paste

3 Tbsp tomato paste

1 tsp dried oregano

2 large carrots, peeled

2 parsnips, peeled

1 celeriac, peeled

2 large onions

5 cloves garlic

vegetable oil for sautéing the
    mushrooms and onions

2 cups water

salt

EWE, GROSS...

Sheep's milk has a grassy (but delicious) flavour that some folks find
a little too much to handle. It will
add some meatiness to the dish
and make the whole thing taste a
little more like the grassy highlands.
If you can't find sheep's milk, try
goat's milk or regular cow's milk.

GET THE POTATOES into a pot, cover with cold water, and get the pot over high heat. Bring to a boil and cook until quite tender. Drain the potatoes and let them dry out a bit.

Put them back in the pot and mash them thoroughly with a potato masher. Add the warm milk, the cold butter, and plenty of salt to taste. It doesn't have to be perfectly smooth, but avoid big huge chunks. Set aside for later.

Meanwhile, prep all the other ingredients. Dice the mushrooms all to about the same size. In a bowl, place the beer, miso, tomato paste, and oregano. Don't worry about mixing them smooth. It's mainly about putting it all together in one place so it's easier later.

Use the large grating hole of a box grater to grate the carrots, parsnips, and celeriac, then place them together in a large bowl. Dice the onions and place in another bowl. Roughly chop the garlic and place in a small bowl.

In a large pot, heat some oil over high heat, toss in the mushrooms, and cook until they lose most of their moisture, about 10 to 12 minutes. Pour in the beer and spice mixture. Cook out the boozy smell, stir until the sauce is nice and smooth, and then transfer the whole mess to a bowl for later.

Get a measuring cup with 2 cups of water ready. Get the same pot you used for the mushrooms over medium heat, and sweat the onions in some oil.

When the onions become beautifully browned, add the garlic and cook until it softens. Then add the grated carrots, parsnip, and celeriac.

This part takes some time. When the bottom of the pot gets browned or things start to stick, just pour in a tiny bit of water and use your wooden spoon to scrape the stuff off the bottom. Cook some more, get the bottom brown again, add some water, and scrape the bottom—so on and so forth. When you have used up half the water, add the mushroom mess as well as the rest of the water because otherwise it will be quite thick. Stir it for a few minutes until it heats through. Add salt to taste, if needed.

Preheat the broiler. Transfer the whole mess to a deep casserole dish, and cover it with a layer of the mashed potatoes. Use a fork to make lines across the surface, then pop it under the broiler for about 8 minutes to get crispy brown.

SERVES A FLOCK OF 8.

the family risotto

First you get the rice, then you get the risotto, and then you get the respect.

Most families have secret recipes. And when your family has as many secrets as this family, it pays to have a little protection. To discover these secret recipes you'll have to show your dedication to the family with lots of hard work and plenty of stirring.

Earn some respect with these killer good risottos.

madonna "big momma" ballzini's risotto and meatballs

You can't get the job done on an empty stomach, so Big Momma makes sure her boys are full with this classic remake of spaghetti and meatballs. She rules the family with an iron fist and a wooden spoon. And if anyone gives her boys any trouble, Big Momma will sort it out quick with her stirring arm.

Big Momma knows it takes balls to run the show.

Meatballs

10 oz ground pork

10 oz ground veal

3 cloves garlic, minced

1 egg

1 Tbsp dried oregano

salt and pepper

vegetable oil for the pan

3 cups tomato sauce

Risotto

6 cups chicken stock

3 Tbsp olive oil

1 white onion, finely chopped

5 cloves garlic, finely minced

2 cups arborio rice

1 cup white wine

8 oz Parmesan, grated

Garnish

1 bunch fresh parsley, chopped

START MAKING YOUR MEATBALLS. In a large mixing bowl, use your hands to thoroughly mix together the ground pork, ground veal, garlic, egg, oregano, and salt and pepper. Form into small, 1-inch round balls and set aside on a plate.

Get 2 large pots and 1 large frying pan on the stove. Fill 1 of the pots with 6 cups of chicken stock, and bring to a simmer.

In the large frying pan, heat some oil over medium heat. Gently place all the meatballs into the hot pan, and cook on all sides until browned all around. Pour in the tomato sauce, and let it all just simmer on low heat while you prepare the risotto.

Place the other pot over medium heat, and sweat the onion and garlic in the olive oil until soft and translucent, using a wooden spoon to stir. Add the arborio, and stir to coat the individual grains with oil. Add the white wine, and stir until the boozy smell evaporates.

Now add 1 ladleful of the simmering chicken stock and stir. When the liquid evaporates a bit and the rice is no longer soupy you can ladle in some more stock.

Continue this progression of ladling and stirring and ladling and stirring until all the stock has been used and the rice is creamy and cooked with just a little bite to it.

To finish the risotto, add half the Parmesan, stirring until smooth.

Serve it in shallow bowls with a saucy scoop of meatballs, and top with parsley and the remaining Parmesan.

SERVES 6 FAMILY MEMBERS.

vinnie "vicious fishes" dimare's risotto with the fishes

In the dark, muddy river in the middle of the night, all the fishes ever get to eat are the bad Italians. They don't know nothing about good Italian.

Speaking of good Italian, try this risotto with fish, fishes, and more fisheses. And you'll avoid being schooled by a gang of sardines—that is, you'd better eat those little vicious fishes before they eat you . . .

Risotto

6 cups fish stock

3 Tbsp olive oil

1 white onion, finely chopped

5 cloves garlic, finely minced

2 cups arborio rice

1 cup white wine

Fishes

¼ cup olive oil

5 anchovy fillets

2 cloves garlic, finely minced

1 lb halibut, cut into cubes the size of the scallops

12 scallops

12 prawns, shells removed

zest and juice of 2 lemons

2 Tbsp capers with caper juice

¼ cup melted butter

1 bunch fresh parsley, chopped

FAIR WARNING

This ain't no amateur-show risotto. This is a pretty labour-intensive job and you are going to have a lot of things going at the same time, so take a look-see and make sure the coast is clear before you start. You might even want to call in a favour and get some help.

GET EVERYTHING IN place in little bowls and stuff. If things aren't neat and organized, you could botch the job.

Now it's time to get to work.

Bring your fish stock up to a simmer.

Get a large pot on the stove over medium, heat the oil, and sweat the onion and garlic until soft and translucent, using a wooden spoon to stir. Add the rice, and stir to coat the individual grains with oil. Add the white wine, and stir until the boozy smell evaporates.

Now add 1 ladleful of the simmering stock, and stir to distribute. When the liquid evaporates a bit and the rice is no longer soupy you can ladle in more stock.

Continue this progression of ladling and stirring and ladling and stirring until all the fish stock has been used and the rice is creamy and cooked with just a little bite to it.

While you are cooking the rice, you will need to simultaneously attend to cooking the fish. It may help to call in a favour.

To start cooking the fish, get a large pan over low heat and start with the olive oil, anchovies, and minced garlic.

When the anchovies have melted and disintegrated, bring the heat up to medium and place the halibut in the pan first. Here's a tip: don't fidget and fuss with the fish, or it will fall apart. Let it cook about 4 minutes, then flip the halibut cubes once. Then immediately place the scallops in the pan, on their flat side. When the scallops are ready to flip (about 2 minutes), do so and crank up the heat to high. Simultaneously add the prawns, lemon juice and zest, capers and caper juice, and butter. When the prawns are cooked (tiger prawns will become pink on both sides), you can toss in the parsley and turn off the heat.

The fish must be served immediately. Spoon out a generous helping of risotto and top with 2 scallops, 2 prawns, and pieces of halibut. Drizzle on some of the pan sauce, and serve to your famished family with a chilled glass of white wine to celebrate a job well done.

SERVES 6 FAMILY MEMBERS WHO WILL EAGERLY GOBBLE UP THE EVIDENCE.

bruno "bloody beets" barbabietola's beets and ricotta risotto

Unless you are lucky enough to have someone like Bruno to do your dirty work, you are going to have to get your own hands dirty with this job. The hours are long, but the result is bloody good risotto, and it will certainly be a good opportunity to prove dedication to the family. When handling the beets, try some rubber gloves or risk getting caught red-handed.

8 tiny red beets, peeled and halved

8 cups water with 2 Tbsp kosher or
  sea salt

3 Tbsp olive oil

1 white onion, finely chopped

3 cloves garlic, finely minced

2 cups arborio rice

1 cup red wine

3 Tbsp butter

splash of red wine vinegar

salt to taste

8 oz ricotta (for homemade ricotta,
  see recipe below)

½ cup toasted pine nuts or
  hazelnuts

fresh-cracked pepper and olive oil

GET 2 LARGE pots on the stove. Put the beet halves in one of the pots and cover with the water and salt. Bring to a boil on high, then reduce to medium heat. Usually you would use stock to make risotto, but the water the beets are cooking in will also act as the risotto's flavour and colour enhancer.

Place the other pot over medium, heat the oil, and sweat the onion and garlic until soft and translucent, using a wooden spoon to stir. Add the arborio and stir to coat the individual grains with oil. Add the red wine, and stir until the boozy smell evaporates.

Now add 1 ladleful of the hot beet-cooking liquid, and stir to distribute. When the liquid evaporates a bit and the rice is no longer soupy you can ladle in more beet water.

Continue this progression of ladling and stirring and ladling and stirring until all the beet water has been used and the rice is creamy and cooked with just a little bite to it.

When all the liquid is ladled out with only the beet left in the pot, add the butter to the pot and sauté until the beets are well covered and glossy. Add a splash of red wine vinegar and a sprinkle of salt to taste.

Serve in shallow bowls with 4 pieces of beet arranged on top, a scoop of ricotta, and a scattering of toasted nuts. Finish it off with a good crack of black pepper and a drizzle of olive oil.

SERVES 6 BLOODY-HUNGRY FAMILY MEMBERS.

MAKING THE RICOTTA

Place 16 cups (4 quarts/4 litres) of whole milk in a large pot and bring to a light simmer (190°F). Add ¼ cup of vinegar (plain white vinegar is the most neutral, but you can use any kind, and even lemon juice) and stir it once. Remove from the heat and put a lid on it. Let it sit for 1 hour.

Place a colander in a large bowl, and line the colander with a double layer of cheesecloth.

In the pot, the milk will have separated into cheese curds. Gently transfer the curds to the colander using a slotted spoon, making sure to get every last ricotta nugget.

Allow the ricotta to drain for at least 1 hour or overnight in the fridge depending on how firm and dry you want it.

Yields approximately 1 lb.

"triple threat" bandiera brothers' tomato, arugula, and parmesan risotto

The notorious Bandiera Brothers were so feared and respected that the Italian flag is named after them ("Bandiera d'Italia"). To show respect to the Italian flag and the Brothers, any food that combines the colours green, white, and red earns the name *Bandiera*.

20 grape tomatoes or cherry tomatoes

2 Tbsp olive oil (for the tomatoes)

6 cups water with 2 Tbsp kosher or sea salt

3 Tbsp olive oil (for the risotto)

1 white onion, finely chopped

5 cloves garlic, finely minced

2 cups arborio rice

1 cup white wine

To finish

8 oz Parmesan, grated

1 clove garlic, grated

a large handful of arugula

fresh-cracked pepper and olive oil

PREHEAT THE OVEN to 400°F. Get all the tomatoes into a baking dish and drizzle on the olive oil and a pinch of salt. Blap them in the oven to roast for 30 minutes while you make the risotto.

Get 2 large pots and 1 medium-to-large frying pan on the stove. Fill 1 pot with the water and salt and bring to a boil. Usually you would use stock to make risotto, but the salt water is just fine for this one. It keeps the dish white, and rest assured there is plenty of flavour from the 6 cloves of garlic.

Place the other pot over medium, heat the oil, and sweat the onion and garlic until soft and translucent, using a wooden spoon to stir. Add the arborio and stir to coat the individual grains with oil. Add the white wine, and stir until the boozy smell has evaporated.

Now add 1 ladleful of the hot salted water, and stir to distribute. When the water evaporates a bit and the rice is no longer soupy you can ladle in more water.

Continue this progression of ladling and stirring and ladling and stirring until all the water has been used and the rice is creamy and cooked with just a little bite to it.

To finish the risotto, add half the Parmesan, a finely grated clove of fresh garlic, and the fresh arugula. Stir until the arugula begins to wilt. Serve the risotto in shallow bowls with the roasted tomatoes and the rest of the Parmesan on top. Finish it off with a good crack of black pepper and a drizzle of olive oil.

SERVES 6 FAMILY MEMBERS.

BANDIERA VERSATILITY

Try some different Bandiera combinations. All you need is something green, something white, and something red.

Green: arugula, spinach, basil

White: any white cheese, white wine, garlic

Red: tomatoes, red peppers, red wine

petey "angry pepper" arrabbiata's spicy sausage and pepper risotto

It makes me so friggin' furious when people try to stiff you with a small portion. What do I look like, some sort of *amuse bouche* . . . some sort of friggin' French mouth amusement to amuse your friggin' face hole?

It's okay to be crazy hungry sometimes. But it's better to fill up with food than to fill up with rage. If you have a burning yearning in your gut, try this hearty risotto of spicy sausage, peppers, and onion with the classic spicy arrabbiata sauce. Enough for yourself and your buddies, and it beats getting a knuckle sandwich in your face hole.

4 cups water

2 cups tomato juice

2 Tbsp kosher or sea salt

1 tsp chili flakes

Sausages and peppers

vegetable oil for the pan

3 large Italian sausages, cut into chunks

1 sweet onion, chopped

1 red pepper, cut into 1-inch chunks

1 yellow pepper, cut into 1-inch chunks

Risotto

3 Tbsp olive oil

1 white onion, finely chopped

2 cloves garlic, finely minced

2 cups arborio rice

1 cup red wine

1 lb Parmesan, grated

fresh-cracked pepper and olive oil

GET 2 LARGE pots and 1 large frying pan on the stove. Fill 1 pot with the water, tomato juice, salt, and chili flakes, and bring to a simmer.

In the frying pan, heat some oil and sauté the sausages and onion over medium-low heat. When they begin to brown, add the peppers, and reduce the heat so it cooks slowly while you make the risotto. If they start to get too brown, add some water to drop the temperature immediately and reduce the heat even more.

Place the other pot over medium, heat the oil, and sweat the onion and garlic until soft and translucent, using a wooden spoon to stir. Add the arborio, and stir to coat the individual grains of rice with oil. Add the red wine, and stir until the boozy smell evaporates.

Now add 1 ladleful of the tomato water, and stir to distribute. When the liquid evaporates a bit and the rice is no longer soupy you can ladle in more tomato water.

Continue this progression of ladling and stirring and ladling and stirring until all the water has been used and the rice is creamy and cooked with just a little bite to it.

To finish the risotto, add half the Parmesan, and stir until smooth and creamy. Scoop a generous helping into each shallow bowl, and top with the sausages and peppers.

Finish it off with a good crack of pepper, the rest of the Parmesan, and a drizzle of olive oil.

SERVES 6 FAMILY MEMBERS.

piña colada panna cotta

You don't have to scour last-minute deals to get the cheapest tropical holiday. Here's an all-inclusive tropical vacation package available no matter where you live, and you don't have to make sure your hepatitis shots are up to date.

First, crank up the heat in your apartment. Go out and pick up a bottle of rum, a coconut bikini, some canned tropical fruit, some tiki masks for your pets, and summa thems lil' umbrellies. Throw a towel on the carpet, lie back, and enjoy this kitschy and canned tropical-island experience that you'll never forget.

1 regular can (14 oz) coconut milk

1 packet gelatin

1 large (30 oz) can crushed
   pineapple

3 Tbsp sugar

½ tsp salt

2 oz shot (¼ cup) rum

¼ cup shredded sweetened coconut
   for garnish

4 tiny umbrellas

PLAN YOUR TRIP early so this dish has time to firm up in the refrigerator and you have time to cover your apartment with tropical kitsch.

Pour $1/3$ cup of the coconut milk into a 2-cup measuring cup, sprinkle in the gelatin, and mix with a fork to disperse the gelatin. Bring the remaining coconut milk to a boil in a small pot. Pour the hot coconut milk over the gelatin mixture. Mix for 1 minute so the gelatin dissolves completely. Divide it evenly into 4 clear glasses, leaving plenty of room for adding the pineapple later. Place the glasses in the fridge and let them firm up for at least 2 hours.

In the meantime, put on some ukulele tunes. When the coconut jelly is set, you can start to prepare the pineapple.

Get a large frying pan onto medium-high heat and sprinkle in the sugar evenly. Don't stir it or move it; the sugar will begin to brown and eventually melt to a smooth liquid. When it is completely melted and slightly brown, add your pineapple, including all the juices in the can, and toss it to coat with the lovely sticky caramel. It may clump up but will melt nicely when it heats through. Crank it to high heat, and let it bubble to reduce the liquid, about 10 minutes.

Get a long match or barbecue lighter ready. Remove the pan from the heat and add the rum, but place the pan immediately back on the heat. Light it, and stand back while the pineapple flambés (catches on fire). When the fire subsides, divide the pineapple evenly among the glasses of coconut jelly.

Top with the shredded coconut and a tiny umbrella, and invite your friends after they get out of work for the day to enjoy your holiday with you. (It's important to eat this right away while the pineapple is hot and the jelly is still cold.)

SERVES YOU AND 3 FRIENDS, OR JUST YOU 4 TIMES.

half-baked pot brownie

Like, hey . . . dudes. Do you need to make something deliciously righteous? Just wrap your head around the concept of a brownie that you mix and bake in one pot. Did that just blow your mind?

Dude, just wait until you try this gooey, fudgy brownie with a sticky-icky centre like a molten chocolate cake. I guarantee your mooching buds will be rolling around looking for freebies when they catch a whiff of this righteous brownie.

4 oz bittersweet chocolate

½ cup sugar

½ cup cold unsalted butter, in pieces

2 large eggs

½ cup flour

¼ cup cocoa powder

¼ tsp salt

PREHEAT THE OVEN to 350°F.

In a medium-sized pot—with a metal handle, not plastic, so the whole thing can go into the oven—melt the chocolate over low heat. As soon as the chocolate melts, remove the pot from the heat.

Add the sugar, and mix with a wooden spoon until grainy but incorporated. Add the cold butter a bit at a time while you continue to mix.

Add 1 egg at a time and mix until smooth.

Sift together the flour, cocoa powder, and salt in a separate bowl. Add the dry mixture directly to the pot a third at a time, stirring after each addition. Use a spatula to scrape down the sides of the pot so nothing burns on the edges, and blap the whole thing into the oven for 35 to 40 minutes. It will still be nice and gooey in the middle. If you want it to be more firm, bake for another 5 to 10 minutes.

Let the brownies cool on the stovetop . . . Be careful not to let anyone touch the hot pot handle.

To serve you can either use a big spoon to scoop out individual servings, or if you got the major munchies you can clean out the pot all by yourself with a little spoon.

food you eat with a

fork

No one is going to just fork over their steak—they'll just tell you to go fork yourself. So if you want to snag something off someone else's plate, use your fork. A spoon is clumsy, a knife is dangerous, and a hand is messy.

Forks are fast as lightning, which is why they call it fork lightning.

snails in the garden

Chefs like to say what grows together, goes together. Crops that share the same sun usually make great flavour partners. Tomatoes and basil, strawberries and rhubarb, lettuce and snails . . .

For some this may be a tough one to swallow, but the best thing to have on your salad is the same thing you spend hours trying to keep off the lettuce in your garden. Put your disdain to rest and get a handle on your ick-factor long enough to try this incredibly edible combination.

crunchy escargot
with aioli slime on fresh garden greens

Aioli slime

1 egg yolk

1 tsp Dijon mustard

²/₃ cup olive oil

1 clove garlic, finely grated or
   minced

zest and juice of 1 lemon

salt to taste

Preparing the escargot

1 can of escargot (approx
   24 escargot)

4 cups water

1 glass of white wine

2 Tbsp white wine vinegar

handful of parsley stems

2 bay leaves

1 rib of celery, chopped

1 carrot, chopped

½ onion, sliced

pinch each salt and pepper

Deep-frying the escargot

1 cup flour

2 eggs, beaten

½ cup breadcrumbs (panko crumbs
   if you got 'em)

canola oil for deep-frying

salt

For when it's time to eat

mixed greens and edible flowers,
   preferably fresh from your garden

FOR THE AIOLI SLIME:

Start with a clean bowl, and vigorously whisk the egg yolk and Dijon mustard together. Continue whisking steadily while very carefully adding the olive oil 1 drop at a time—try pouring oil into a spoon, then adding the oil drop by drop from the spoon into the bowl. This will start the emulsion, and it should begin to thicken and start looking like mayonnaise. Continue to whisk, drizzling the oil slowly and in a very thin stream this time. When half the oil is incorporated you can pour the rest in a little faster than before (but not too fast).

The result should be a thick, gloopy mayonnaise. To make the slime delicious, add the garlic and the lemon juice and zest, and season to taste. Transfer to a smaller bowl, cover, and place in the fridge while the flavours develop and you get your escargot going.

FOR THE ESCARGOT:

Escargot from a can are already cleaned, but if you cook them briefly in a quick stock, it will make them extra tasty, not to mention give you a little peace of mind. Place all the ingredients except the escargot in a medium-sized pot and bring to a boil over high heat. As soon as it boils, add the escargot, remove from the heat, and allow to steep for 10 minutes. Remove the escargot, discarding the stock, and set the escargot aside on a paper towel to dry.

You'll need 3 bowls for the dredging. In the first put the flour, in the second the beaten eggs, and in the last one the breadcrumbs.

Drop a few of the escargot in the flour, and toss until they are evenly and lightly coated. Next, move them into the beaten egg for a quick dunk before you finish them in the breadcrumbs. Make sure at each dredging station that the escargot are evenly coated.

You can either whip out your deep-fryer or deep-fry using a fairly deep pot. Whatever you do, bring up the canola oil to 350°F.

Deep-fry the little snail nuggets until golden brown, and set aside on a paper towel. Salt them liberally while they are still hot, but let them cool down a bit before serving.

To serve, lay down a bed of garden greens, scatter in some crunchy escargot, and liberally drizzle with aioli slime.

SELL OUT CORN

The sisters have gone through rough times since industrial agriculture lured corn away for the glitz and glam of high-yield farming. Since it is virtually impossible to find genetically unmodified corn, growing your own three-sisters garden could be a great way to get some spiritual harmony back into your life via your food source.

three sisters succotash salad

According to an ancient Iroquois agricultural system, three inseparable sisters have been in the garden for a long time—corn, beans, and squash, growing together in perfect harmony. A stalk of corn grows straight-up tall, the bean vine weaves up the corn stalk, and the squash grows on the ground to keep the weeds down. Whether or not you are a proficient urban gardener, find harmony with the Iroquois spirit sisters with this fresh salad.

Vinaigrette

3 Tbsp white wine vinegar or lemon
   juice

1 Tbsp Dijon mustard

2 cloves garlic, crushed

pinch of salt

a crank or two of pepper

½ cup olive oil

The sisters

1 cup freshly shucked fava beans
   (canned is fine, though)

2 ears of corn, husks removed

4 small to medium zucchini (forget
   about the big ones, they're
   spongy)

Friendly visitors

Add 1 or more of these ingredients
   to add some glam to your salad:

grated carrot for colour

diced red pepper for sweetness

freshly chopped herbs like thyme,
   mint, basil, and/or chives

PLACE ALL THE VINAIGRETTE ingredients in a jar with a sealable lid. Now, put the lid on tight and shake it like you are playing an instrument . . . a maraca, not a piano or a guitar. Set it aside. Making it a day ahead is good, but an hour is fine.

If you're using fresh lima beans, get them into a pot, cover in cold water (no salt), and bring to a boil. Reduce to a simmer and cook for 25 minutes or until tender. When they are done, cool them in a colander under cold running water. Drain and toss in a little vinaigrette, and let them marinate for an hour or so. (If using canned lima beans, rinse well before marinating.)

Since you are in the garden, you might as well fire up the outside grill for the corn. Get the grill super-hot, and grill the corn all the way around. Let it cool before you trim off all the kernels with a sharp paring knife.

For the zucchini, use your vegetable peeler to peel off long ribbons from top to bottom on 1 side. When you reach the seeds in the middle, stop and rotate the zucchini and start on another side. Don't worry too much about getting the ribbons to be the same width—just try to get them long, and avoid the seeds. When you are done, you should have a lovely pile of ribbons with an intact zucchini core left behind. You won't be cooking the zucchini; you'll be eating it raw and it will taste lovely, crunchy, and sweet.

Pile the ribbons in a bowl and drizzle with enough dressing just to coat, tossing with your fingertips and separating the ribbons so they start to pile up nice and high.

To serve, fill up a big serving bowl with loads of bouncy springy zucchini ribbons, and sprinkle them with the lima beans, grilled corn, any of the friendly visitors, and a good drizzle of dressing. Eat it in the garden with your sisters, some baguettes, and a bottle of chilly white wine.

colossal squid salad

The kraken was a mythical squid-like sea monster that supposedly attacked wooden ships. But modern research has discovered giant squids to be real. There's a cephalopod actually dubbed the "giant squid," and something even scarier: the "colossal squid." This monster can be 14 metres long with a proportionately larger mantle, and frightening swivel hooks on its attack tentacles that are straight out of a deep-sea sci-fi thriller. They would produce calamari the size of a big rig tire . . . and probably just as easy to chew.

So consider eating them before they eat you. This bright summer salad is a great way to keep those little squiddies from growing up and plucking you off the beach like a kid reaching for a cookie on the counter.

Vinaigrette

2 oranges

1 Tbsp white wine vinegar

½ cup olive oil

1 shallot

2 cloves garlic

1 fresh hot chili (optional)

salt and fresh-cracked pepper

Salad

8 fingerling potatoes or 6 small new
   potatoes

1 lb baby squid (approx 12), cleaned
   (see sidebar below)

olive oil to coat the squid

salt and pepper

1 bunch fresh mint, leaves only

½ bunch fresh parsley, leaves only

½ cup toasted whole almonds,
   crushed

S'GUID ENOUGH TO EAT

Ideally you can get your squid already cleaned with the legs and mantles separated. But if all you can get is whole squid, you will have to make sure you clean them properly. If frozen, first thaw them completely.

The trick is to not rupture the ink sac. First remove the quill (bone) by working your fingertips into the mantle near the head and pulling it out toward the tentacles. Then hold the tip of the mantle steady, and pull the cluster of legs downward. The guts should all come loose, including the ink sac. Finally you can pull the wings off of the mantle and peel off the rest of the coloured membranous skin. Now you will have a perfectly white, perfectly smooth squid mantle.

Slice the guts away from the tentacles and feel around for a hard little nub. It's the beak, the hardest part of an otherwise soft little invertebrate. Cut out that hard piece or potentially suffer a broken tooth.

BEFORE YOU GET cooking, make the vinaigrette so the flavours have time to evolve and get bigger. Start by zesting half of the first orange into a medium bowl using a grater or Microplane, making sure not to get any of the bitter white part. Juice the 2 oranges into the bowl. Whisk in the vinegar and the olive oil.

Finely mince the shallot, crush the garlic with your palm or the flat side of your knife, and split the chili pepper in half. Toss them all into the bowl. Season with salt and pepper. Pour the vinaigrette into a jar with a tight-fitting lid and set aside.

Cut the potatoes into bite-sized pieces (if you're using fingerlings, just halve them) and put them in a pot of cold water. Bring to a boil and let them simmer gently until tender. Drain them in a colander, and allow them to air dry and cool down to room temperature.

Fire up the grill to a scorching high heat, warming it up for at least 10 minutes while you lube up the squid.

In a small bowl, toss the cleaned whole mantles and tentacles in olive oil to coat, and season with some salt and pepper. Although it's not necessary, it'll make grilling easy if you jab the squids onto skewers. (Leave about ½ inch between pieces.)

Grill them for approximately 3 minutes on each side. Don't overcook them or they will get tough and rubbery. When they are nicely marked by the grill, transfer to a plate and allow them to sit until cool enough to handle. With a sharp knife, cut the mantle into rings and the tentacle clusters in half.

Toss the potatoes, squid, mint, and parsley into a bowl. Shake up the vinaigrette in the lidded jar, and dress the salad with half the vinaigrette. (You can discard the chili pepper and garlic clove.) Toss carefully but thoroughly with your hands. Taste and add more vinaigrette if needed, and adjust the seasoning.

Transfer to a nice serving platter, and top with the toasted almonds.

SERVES 4 TO 6 PEOPLE OR 1 COLOSSAL PERSON.

mussels make the man

Forget about maxing out your bench press or doing another set of reverse-transabdominal-Romanian-skull-crushers. If you want to impress the bodacious babes at the beach, don't bother getting buffed in the gym. Show them your crazy-cool skills with a finger-licking (and surprisingly simple) mussel recipe.

These mussels will make you the King of the Beach.

CHECK OUT YOUR MUSSELS

Here are two rules for mussel safety.

1. Keep it tight

Fresh mussels will be closed tight. Or if they're slightly open, they should close up tight when you tap them on the counter. If you encounter a raw mussel that won't close easily, toss it.

2. Max it out

For cooked mussels the opposite rule applies—they should have opened on their own and opened wide. You should never have to pry open a cooked mussel. If you encounter a closed one, toss that one too.

MUSSEL PREP TALK

You can't expect to just start hitting the mussels hard right away. When you bring home your mussels, keep them in an empty bowl with a damp towel on top and store in the fridge. Never place them in something airtight or in water or you will kill them. Good mussels should be barnacle free, but sometimes they need a little scrub to get the barnacles off. Finally, before you cook them, check for little beards—nobody likes unsightly body hair and they are unpleasantly chewsome. Give the beards a good tug to rip them right out of the mussels. Now your mussels are looking good enough to eat.

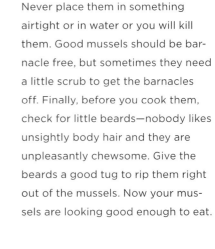

mussels from brussels

2 lb fresh mussels
3 slices bacon, diced
1 shallot, minced
6 cloves roasted garlic (see
  page 73)
1 bottle of light-coloured beer
1 tsp dried tarragon
1 lemon, cut into wedges

PUT DICED BACON in a large cold pot with a lid. Then get the pot over medium-low heat to render the fat from the bacon. Stir occasionally and make sure the bacon does not burn. When it's crispy, remove it and place on a paper towel.

In the remaining bacon fat sweat the shallot and roasted garlic just for 30 seconds or so. Crank the heat all the way up. Glug in the beer and let the foam disappear while you scrape the brown bits off the bottom. Add the tarragon.

Now toss in your mussels and get the lid on. Shake them around, and after about 2 minutes check to see if the mussels are opening. Once they have all opened, toss mussels and all into individual bowls (or 1 big bowl if serving 2—see below). When you pour out the lovely cooking liquid, spoon or pour from the top to leave behind any grit or sediment that may have collected at the bottom.

Top with the crispy bacon, and serve with lemon wedges, beer, and bread on the side.

french coast

2 lb fresh mussels
2 Tbsp cold butter
1 shallot, minced or sliced
2 cloves garlic, roughly chopped
1 glass of white wine
handful of fresh parsley, chopped
fresh-cracked pepper

GET A LARGE POT with a lid on high heat. Toss in the butter, let it foam, and add the shallot and garlic.

Just before they brown (about 15 seconds), add the wine. Bring to a boil, and toss in your mussels. Get the lid on the pot. Shake them around, and after about 2 minutes, check to see if the mussels are opening. Once they have all opened, toss everything that's in the pot into a serving bowl (or bowls), and top with the parsley and fresh-cracked pepper. When you pour out the lovely cooking liquid, spoon or pour from the top to leave behind any grit or sediment that may have collected at the bottom.

Serve with chunks of French baguette to sop up every drop.

greecey mussels

2 lb fresh mussels
2 Tbsp olive oil
1 fennel bulb, finely sliced
zest and juice of 1 lemon
10 pitted kalamata olives
1 tsp dried oregano
2 oz shot (¼ cup) ouzo (or
  sambuca)
½ cup crumbled feta

GET A LARGE POT with a lid on medium heat. Glug in the olive oil, add the fennel, and cook until softened.

Crank up the heat all the way. Throw in the lemon zest and juice, olives, oregano, and booze. Cook out the boozy smell, then toss in the mussels. Get the lid on. Shake them around and check to see if the mussels are opening. Once they have all opened, toss everything that's in the pot in a big bowl (or bowls), and top with feta cheese. When you pour out the lovely cooking liquid, spoon or pour from the top to leave behind any grit or sediment that may have collected at the bottom.

Serve with chunks of pita brushed with some olive oil and grilled quickly.

TWO-SOME OR MORE-SOME

These recipes will serve two for a main meal or four for a starter. If you are serving two, just use one bowl to make the experience more hands-on. And remember, too many napkins will inhibit finger licking.

cheesy mac's mac and cheese

Here is a surefire way for single dudes to impress the ladies.

First, all you need are some cheesy mac-daddy pickup lines. And then when you get her back to your place seal the deal by making some mac and cheese.

The secret to successful cheesy mac pickup lines or cheesy mac and cheese: the cheesier the better. Works every time!

6 oz cheese with body—cheddar,
  Gruyère

3 oz soft cheese—brie, Camembert

3 oz hard cheese—Parmesan,
  Asiago, Grana Padano

1 oz stinky cheese—blue cheese,
  smoked cheese

1 Tbsp butter (more for the
  breadcrumb topping)

1 Tbsp flour

1 ½ cups milk, warmed up

1 tsp dried yellow mustard

2 cups dried macaroni

salt for the pasta water

3 Tbsp melted butter

½ cup dry breadcrumbs

HAVE ALL YOUR ingredients measured out before you start. Because when it comes to fancy-pants cooking, it's all about fancy little bowls for the ingredients. Weigh your cheese and grate or crumble it (or vice versa), and set it out in a bowl. The fancy pants are optional.

Preheat the oven to broil.

Get a large pot of water going on high heat for the pasta. And get another large pot over medium-high heat. Toss in the 1 Tbsp of butter, and just as it melts sprinkle in the flour, mixing with a whisk. When the two are clumpy but incorporated add a little bit of the warm milk while whisking continuously. When the mixture is thick and smooth, add a little more milk while whisking, continuing to add more and more milk each time until you've poured in all of it. Keep stirring as the mixture comes to a boil, and then turn down the heat to medium-low. Whisk in the mustard.

By now the water should be boiling. Add some salt and toss in the macaroni. Now back to the sauce. Add the grated cheese a bit at a time, stirring so it stays smooth.

Cook your macaroni until it is al dente, then drain it in a colander. Toss the pasta into the sauce and stir it all up. Transfer the mess into a baking dish.

In a small bowl, thoroughly combine the breadcrumbs with the 3 Tbsp of melted butter. Sprinkle the breadcrumb mix over the top of the macaroni. Blap it in the oven for just a few minutes, until the breadcrumbs get golden and crispy on top.

Take the macaroni out of the oven, and let it sit for 10 minutes to cool down before you, er, heat things up.

Turn down the lights and turn up the cheese.

CHEESY PICKUP LINES FOR YOU TO TRY

If I could rearrange the alphabet, I'd put U and I together.

If I said you had a nice body, would you hold it against me?

You have an onion booty. It is making me cry.

Do you want to be the little spoon?

If I had a dollar for every girl I'd seen as hot as you, I'd have one dollar.

I'm so sweet, I go straight to your hips.

Bonus pickup line: If you were words on a page, you would be the fine print.

angel hair conditioner pasta

As any angel will attest, flying around all day wreaks havoc on your hair. However, it does not take very much to unfrazzle after a long day if you have angel hair . . . angel hair pasta, that is.

Making dinner is fast and easy with this recipe, which turns light delicate pasta into something rich and luxurious with just a few simple ingredients. Try the other treatment options if you would like to try something new with your hair.

salt for the pasta water

½ lb dried vermicelli pasta

1 cup Greek yogurt

1 clove garlic, grated

1 Tbsp olive oil

½ cup grated Asiago

1 Tbsp lemon juice

salt

loads of fresh-cracked pepper

MAKE SURE YOU have all your ingredients in place before you cook the pasta, because you will need to work quickly once the pasta is drained.

Bring a pot of water to a boil, using lots of water so the pasta doesn't get tangled up—you want to avoid a bad hair day. Salt it heavily. Cook the pasta, and taste for doneness after 4 minutes. If it isn't al dente, check frequently until it is.

Drain the pasta in a colander, setting aside some of the cooking water. Get the pasta right back into the same pot.

Return the pot to the same element, but turn it off. (The remaining heat will cook everything through.) Now quickly add the yogurt, garlic, and olive oil, tossing gently until the hair is evenly coated and luxurious. Add some of the cooking water if you think the sauce needs it. Finally, toss in the Asiago and lemon juice (plus any of the treatment options below), and stir just until the cheese is incorporated and starting to melt. Salt if needed.

Get a big tong full of hair into a big bowl, then top with loads of fresh-cracked pepper.

HAIR TREATMENTS

Frosty tips: lemon zest, which adds brightness and pizzazz

Red highlights: thin slices of sun-dried tomatoes

Blond streaks: a pinch of saffron added to the yogurt, for streaky colour

More volume: thin strips of prosciutto, for richness

Something different: fresh arugula, for an unusual choice of hair colour.

It works beautifully with the pasta!

puttanesca pastitute

Puttanesca is derived from the Italian word *putta*, meaning "prostitute." Fast, cheap, and pungent . . . The saucy prostitutes of Naples are famous for their pasta, said to lure customers with its intoxicating aromas.

This sauce combines the strong flavours of garlic, chili flakes, anchovies, capers, and olives—hot, spicy, and like an invigorating mouth spanking. For any working girl (. . . or boy), this pantry-raiding recipe is easy to make at a moment's notice, especially if you only have a few minutes between jobs. It leaves you plenty of time to freshen up and load on the mascara . . . and remember that good girls pinch, whores use blush.

salt for the pasta water

1 lb dried spaghetti

¼ cup olive oil

3-5 anchovy fillets

3 cloves garlic, minced

1 shallot, minced

1 tsp chili flakes

1 small can (14 oz) diced tomatoes

2 Tbsp tomato paste

20 kalamata olives, pitted

1 Tbsp capers

½ bunch fresh parsley, chopped

8 oz Parmesan, grated

BRING A BIG POT of water to a boil. Salt it generously . . . salty like the Mediterranean Sea.

While the water is coming to a boil, get a large frying pan on low heat. Pour in the olive oil, and gently lay down the anchovy fillets. Warm them up slowly until they start to melt and fall apart. Add the garlic, shallot, and chili flakes. It won't take long for your eyes to well up with tears . . . but grow up, this is no time for crying.

If the water is boiling, you should toss in the pasta.

When the shallot is soft, turn the heat all the way up and add the tomatoes and tomato paste. Take the tomato can and use it to scoop out half a can of pasta water, and add it to the pan. The starches in the water will add nice body to the sauce. Continue bubbling so the sauce is reduced but still slightly sloppy.

Toward the end of the cooking time, add the olives and capers.

Drain your al dente pasta. Pour the sauce into the now empty pot, then transfer the pasta back in to mix it all up.

Serve with loads of parsley and grated Parmesan.

SERVES 4 HARD-WORKING GIRLS OR BOYS.

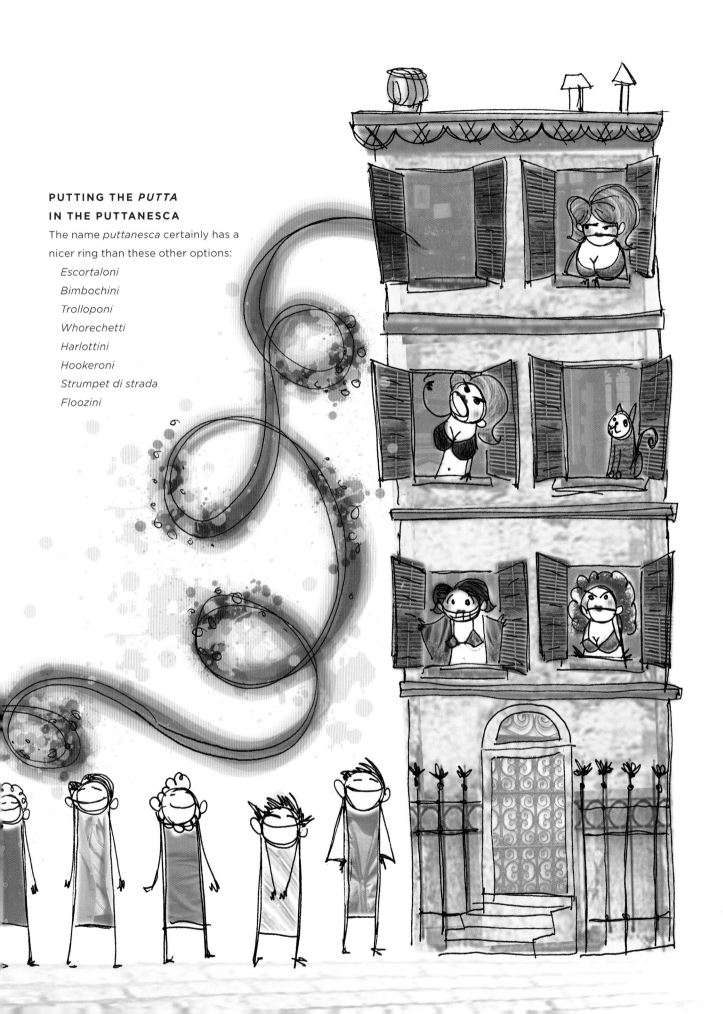

PUTTING THE *PUTTA*
IN THE PUTTANESCA

The name *puttanesca* certainly has a
nicer ring than these other options:

> *Escortaloni*
>
> *Bimbochini*
>
> *Trolloponi*
>
> *Whorechetti*
>
> *Harlottini*
>
> *Hookeroni*
>
> *Strumpet di strada*
>
> *Floozini*

nipply gnudist

Frigid weather means an inhibiting change of wardrobe for nudists. Uninhibit yourself from your constrictive long undies and keep your tender bits warm from the inside out.

Tender little gnudi pasta dumplings are easy to prepare, but they take some extra time to form in the fridge. The result will be well worth the wait when you take your first bite of these yummy little bundles of warmth.

Fill up on warm-fuzzy feeling, then head outside to go for a bare-rump romp in the snow. But you may want some strategically placed muffs to keep Jack Frost from nipping at your nipply bits.

saucy nibbly gnudi

10 oz ricotta (see page 39 for
   homemade ricotta)

4 oz Parmesan, grated

1 egg

¼ tsp salt

4 cups semolina flour

¼ cup butter

2 cloves garlic, smooshed

5 sage leaves

1 Tbsp balsamic vinegar

1 oz Parmesan, grated

fresh-cracked pepper

IN A BOWL, mix together the ricotta, Parmesan, egg, and salt until smooth.

Fill a straight-sided dish with half of the semolina flour. Place the ricotta bowl next to the semolina dish. Take a spoonful of the ricotta mixture and roll it in your palms to make a perfect ball. This is good practice for making snowballs. Place the balls in the bed of semolina flour with space between each ball.

When you are finished rolling all the ricotta balls, cover them with the remaining semolina flour, cover with plastic wrap, and place in the fridge for 48 to 72 hours. The semolina flour will extract the moisture from the ricotta and form its own natural pasta shell. The shell is delicate and requires gentle handling and cooking.

To cook, fill a pot with 2 inches of salty water and bring to a very gentle simmer. A rapid boil will tear the gnudi to shreds.

Carefully extract the tender little dumplings from their semolina nest and gingerly shake off the excess flour.

Get a frying pan over medium-low heat. To make a fake quickie brown-butter sauce, melt the butter with the smooshed garlic and sage leaves. Just when the butter begins to brown, remove the pan from the heat and swirl in the balsamic vinegar.

Place a few gnudi in the gently simmering water and cook for 5 minutes. Remove them with a slotted spoon; don't dump them into a strainer or they will fall apart. Place the gnudi directly on a warm plate.

The sage and garlic are certainly edible, but they are mainly here for flavour so avoid serving them on the gnudi.

Serve 8 gnudi per person. Drizzle generously with brown-butter sauce and top with a sprinkling of Parmesan and cracked pepper.

FEEDS 4 PEOPLE, BUT EXPECT TO WANT TO MAKE THEM AGAIN IMMEDIATELY . . . OH WAIT, THEY TAKE 2 DAYS TO MAKE. BETTER MAKE MORE NEXT TIME.

NIBBLE COVERINGS

It would be in poor taste to cover these tender little gnudi with anything heavy.

Keep the sauces light and skimpy. A little cream sauce or a dab of tomato sauce goes a long way and makes a nice complement to the gnudi. Make sure not to cover them completely or they just wouldn't be gnudi.

the tale of mr. b. russell sprout

Once upon a time there was a gentleman named Mr. B. Russell Sprout who lived in a red-brick townhouse on a cobblestone lane near the bank where he worked. Even the other bankers thought Mr. Sprout was an old fuddy-duddy because he always wore the same limp green tweed suit and bowler hat every day.

Nobody ever invited him round for dinner, fearing he would be a dreadful bore.

One day after work, Mr. Sprout joined his colleagues for a pint at the pub.

A few pints later, he had taken off his stuffy old suit (along with everything else) and was running around town making a spectacular spectacle of himself. He definitely knew how to party. After that night, Mr. Sprout was invited round for dinner all over town, and everyone was happy to see him . . . especially after they got a little booze in him.

saur sprout

10 Brussels sprouts
5 dried juniper berries
2 oz shot (¼ cup) gin
1 cup water
¼ cup white vinegar (any kind)
2 tsp sugar
big pinch of salt
2 Tbsp butter

SHRED THE BRUSSELS sprouts like they were little cabbages. Toss them in a small pot with the juniper berries, gin (booze made with juniper berries), water, vinegar, sugar, and salt. Bring up the whole mess to a gentle simmer over medium-high heat, and let it just bubble for a while until it is all softened and most of the moisture has evaporated, about 15 minutes. Add the butter at the end, stirring until it melts.

Serve this one with turkey smokies and some mustard.

SERVES 2.

SPROUTSICLES
Here is a trick from the old country. Toss your Brussels sprouts in the snow . . . or the freezer. Freezing cabbages and Brussels sprouts breaks down the tough tissues, making for easier, more enjoyable chewing. Babushka grannies use this trick for cabbage rolls.

brussels beer fest

1 head of roasted garlic (see recipe below)
5 slices double-smoked bacon
10 frozen Brussels sprouts (see sidebar below)
1 bottle of light-coloured beer
salt and pepper to taste

SLAP YOUR BACON into a big cold frying pan. Get the pan on medium heat and cook the bacon until it is crispy, then place it on a paper towel–lined plate. If you are a raving fatophobe you can drain the excess bacon fat (but really, that would be crazy). When cool, cut the bacon into bits.

Crank up the heat all the way and toss in the Brussels sprouts whole. Shimmy them around so they get nicely browned all over, for 2 minutes. Add the beer, the roasted garlic, and a pinch of salt. Keep cooking (and occasionally shimmy) on high until the liquid evaporates and a little syrupy sauce is left at the bottom of the pan, about 10 to 15 minutes. Season to taste with salt and pepper.

Serve in a big bowl and top with the crispy crumbled bacon on top.

SERVES 2.

ROASTED GARLIC
Preheat the oven to 400°F. Trim off the pointy top of a head of garlic to expose the cloves. Drizzle with oil, sprinkle with salt, wrap it in foil, and blap it in the oven for 30 to 35 minutes. When cool, squeeze out the cloves.

brussels meet brandy

10 Brussels sprouts, halved
pinch of salt
2 Tbsp butter, divided
1 oz shot (2 Tbsp) brandy
juice and zest of 1 orange
1 shallot, minced
sprig of fresh thyme (leaves only)
¼ cup dried cranberries

PLACE THE BRUSSELS sprout halves flat side down in a frying pan. Cover halfway with cold water, and add a pinch of salt and 1 Tbsp of butter. Place the pan on high heat, and cook at a rip-roaring boil until almost all the water has evaporated.

To flambé the sprouts without lighting yourself on fire, carefully remove the pan from the heat, add the shot of brandy, and, using a long match or a barbecue lighter, light the booze on fire and place the pan back on the heat. When the fire subsides, add the orange juice and zest, shallot, thyme leaves, dried cranberries, and the last 1 Tbsp of butter all at the same time. Toss and cook for a couple more minutes until the sauce gets syrupy and glossy.

Make everyone try at least one. It will make them change their minds about Brussels sprouts.

SERVES 2.

totally-baked-out-of-their-minds potatoes

Dude, the next time you and your couch potato buds decide to do some "baking," roll a fat batch of these sticky-icky-green stuffed baked potatoes. You can stash them in little baggies in your freezer for the next time you have the munchies, and then fire up one or two of these in the oven straight from the freezer. Remember to set a timer so you don't forget it's in the oven . . . that'd be the bad kinda "burning."

4 large russet potatoes

1 package frozen . . . not freshy . . . spinach

3 cups grated Emmenthal or white cheddar cheese

1 Tbsp butter

1 Tbsp flour

1 cup milk

1 tsp dried oregano . . . not the fake stuff

salt and pepper

CHRONIC LIAR?

Okay, I have to say I'm not actually a pothead. I'm just faking the lingo to sound cool.

I admit I did "smoke the pot" once, but it was in BC, so it doesn't count 'cause that's equivalent to jaywalking. I coughed so much, I decided to save myself the embarrassment of ever smoking up again by quitting cold turkey right then and there.

PREHEAT THE OVEN to 350°F.

Wash the potatoes and prick them all over with a fork. Then pop them in the oven straight onto the middle rack. They should take at least 1 hour . . . so set a timer and go play your video games. The potatoes are done when you insert a sharp knife and there is no resistance. After you take out the hot-as-hell potatoes from the oven, let them cool down for another half hour of video games.

Cut the potatoes in half lengthwise and scoop out the insides into a big friggin' bowl. Don't scoop out all the white part, just most of it. You'll be filling in the skins later. Mash the potato with the potato masher—you know, the great weapon of choice in your backyard wrestling ring.

Now get the frozen spinach into the microwave and nuke it for about 5 minutes to thaw. Meanwhile, grate the cheese, get the butter and flour ready to go, and measure out the milk.

Okay, this is going to take some concentration, a whisking of at least 3 minutes straight. Get a pot on medium-high heat. Drop in the butter right away and sprinkle in the flour. Now use a whisk to mix the melting butter and the flour. They will bunch up pretty quick, which is cool. Keep whisking and pour in a splash of milk. Holy crap, it looks like gross goo, that's cool, keep stirring. Pour in some more milk. Holy crap, still gross, it's cool, keep stirring and make sure it stays smooth. Go a little more on the milk and keep stirring . . . Still looks like pus, but that's fine as long as it's smooth. Now you can dump in the rest of the milk and keep stirring until it comes to a boil.

When it boils, turn off the heat and switch to a wooden spoon. Stir in 2 cups of the cheese a bit at a time until it's smooth. Save the other cup of cheese for the topping. Then plus it with some oregano, salt, and pepper.

Finally you can dump in the thawed spinach . . . don't worry about draining the liquid, nothing wrong with a little murky green water. Mix it all up, then pour all of it onto the mashed potatoes, and mix some more. Now you can start filling up your potato skins. When they are full, smooth out the top and pack some of the leftover cheese on top.

You can bake 'em now, or pack 'em into little baggies and into your freezer for a later date. When you're ready to eat, nuke them for 2 minutes, or preheat the oven to 300°F, toss them on a baking sheet, and bake for 45 minutes or until they are heated through and crispy on top.

It sure beats the hell out of a bag of discount stale chips.

WILL FEED 4 HUNGRY STONERS OR 8 REGULAR PEOPLE.

inter-rootial marriages

Walls of prejudice are coming down, but we still have a long way to go before they collapse for good. If people keep their roots separate, we will be forced to live in a bland world without knowing the joys of inter-rootial marriages.

There have been some classic combinations that pioneered miscegenation in the kitchen, but let's give them a whole new twist to keep the love alive and strong.

Carrots and ginger won the world over by being puréed together in a soup. And now they renew their wild and crazy tendencies with a quickie pickle. How's that for keeping the love alive?

Potatoes and celeriac get along smashingly because they are both big and beautiful. While they are quite happy to be mashed together, they are even bolder in a German-style potato-and-celeriac salad.

Beet-and-horseradish has made its mark in British fare as roasted beets roasted with horseradish, but the world will marvel at their sophistication when they are dressed up in a carpaccio.

Let your roots intertwine to create a more colourful existence for one and all. Down with rootial segregation!

celeriac and potato salad

It sure gets cold in the winter. But that shouldn't stop you from going on a romantic picnic. Instead of cold potato salad, pack this German-style potato salad with yummy bacon, potatoes, celeriac, and dill pickles, served warm to keep you snug and satisfied. Cuddle on—or under—a warm fuzzy blanket with a snuggle buddy . . . and don't be surprised if your next picnic is a family picnic.

1 large celeriac

4 large waxy potatoes

3 large dill pickles

1 bunch fresh dill

1 lemon

1 shallot

1 clove garlic

6 slices thick-cut bacon

1 Tbsp vegetable oil

2 Tbsp butter

salt and pepper

2 Tbsp sour cream

1 Tbsp grainy mustard

PEEL THE CELERIAC by cutting off the top and bottom. Lay it on a flat side, and use your big knife to trim the gnarly skin off the sides. Peel your potatoes. Cut the potatoes and celeriac into approximately 1 1/2- to 2-inch cubes. Place them in a large pot and fill it up with cold water. (Do not salt the water.)

Get the pot on high heat, and while it comes to a boil prep the rest of the salad. The celeriac will float to the top, but that's cool.

Cut the pickles into large rounds the size of the potato chunks. Chop the dill. Zest and juice the lemon. Mince the shallots and garlic.

When the water just starts to boil, you can start the bacon. Lay out your 6 slices of bacon in a very large cold pan and set the pan on medium heat. Drizzle in the oil and let the fat render out of the bacon.

Back to the potatoes. Check for doneness by taking out a big piece of potato from the bottom of the pot and cutting it or biting into it. You'll know it needs more cooking if it's raw and crunchy. Don't worry about checking the celeriac, as celeriac a little undercooked is fine, and you can't really overcook it either.

When the potatoes and celeriac are ready, drain them into a colander and let them sit for 10 minutes, until they have released a lot of their excess moisture.

When the bacon is crispy, transfer it to a paper towel–lined plate.

To the bacon fat, add the shallot, garlic, and butter. When the shallot is soft, add the potatoes and celeriac. Toss to coat, and then sprinkle in the lemon juice and zest. Salt and pepper generously. Transfer to a bowl and gently mix in the pickles, dill, sour cream, and mustard. Crumble the bacon and sprinkle it on top.

SERVES YOURSELF AND 7 HUNGRY FRIENDS.

beet carpaccio

It is a romantic rule that opposites attract. The beet is frighteningly red, the horseradish insipidly pale; the beet subtly sweet, the horseradish fiery. In spite of their differences, or more likely because of them, these two roots get along incredibly well.

It may be a little hard to understand, but it is certainly impossible to deny the attraction between beet and horseradish. Love comes in all shapes, sizes, and colours, after all.

4 small to medium red beets
salt for boiling the beets
⅔ cup sour cream or crème fraîche
1 Tbsp prepared horseradish
1 tsp white wine vinegar
salt
5 chives, thinly chopped
¼ cup toasted hazelnuts, crushed
orange zest
drizzle of olive oil
pinch of flaky finishing salt

PLACE THE BEETS in a pot of salted water and bring to a boil. Depending on the size of the beets, they may take anywhere from 30 to 50 minutes of boiling. To check for doneness, stick a skewer into the middle of a beet; when you let go of the beet it should slide off easily.

Run cold water on the beets to cool. When they are cool enough to handle, rub away the skin under running water to avoid bad hand stains.

Put the beets in the refrigerator to chill for at least 30 minutes or overnight.

In a bowl, combine the sour cream or crème fraîche, horseradish, vinegar, a pinch of salt, and half the chopped chives.

The trick to this carpaccio is to slice the beets as thinly and uniformly as possible. Use a mandoline or a long knife to carefully cut perfect thin rounds.

Use the largest plates you have because carpaccio likes to spread out. Start in the middle, and overlap the rounds slightly in a circular pattern so they eventually cover the entire plate.

Now it is time to sparingly apply the flavour toppers. With a spoon, drizzle the horseradish cream all over like it's a minimalist Jackson Pollock painting.

Sprinkle on the rest of the chives and the toasted hazelnuts. Using a zester (ideally a Microplane), just give the orange a couple drags from way up high, so you get just a hint of orange zest all over the plate. Finish with a quick drizzle of olive oil and a crunchy smattering of fancy, flaky finishing salt.

SERVES 2 MODERATELY HUNGRY PEOPLE, BUT YOU CAN STRETCH IT TO 4 AS A STARTER.

carrot-and-ginger quickie pickle

Carrots and ginger have been paired together for a long time. But this monogamy between carrot and ginger can turn quickly to monotony. How do you spice things up? Well, quickies now and then can help any relationship. These quick pickles hardly take any time, but the effects will linger.

3 medium carrots

3 oz knob of ginger, cut into thin slices

2 cups water

1 cup white vinegar (any kind)

1 Tbsp kosher or sea salt

1 Tbsp sugar

USE YOUR PEELER to clean up all the carrots. Then use the peeler to peel off long strips of carrot ribbons. Don't worry about keeping perfectly even widths—just do your best to use up as much of the carrot as you can without shaving any of your fingers. Collect the carrot ribbons in a jar or large bowl.

In a small pot, combine the ginger slices, water, vinegar, salt, and sugar, and bring to a boil until all the sugar and salt have dissolved.

Pour the boiling liquid through a strainer (to catch the ginger) onto the carrots. Make sure all the ribbons are submerged. Simply let them cool down to room temperature. Then move them into the fridge to chill, where they will keep for a couple weeks.

Makes a great flavour-bursting accompaniment to heavy cuts of meat, on tuna sandwiches, or anything else you can think of.

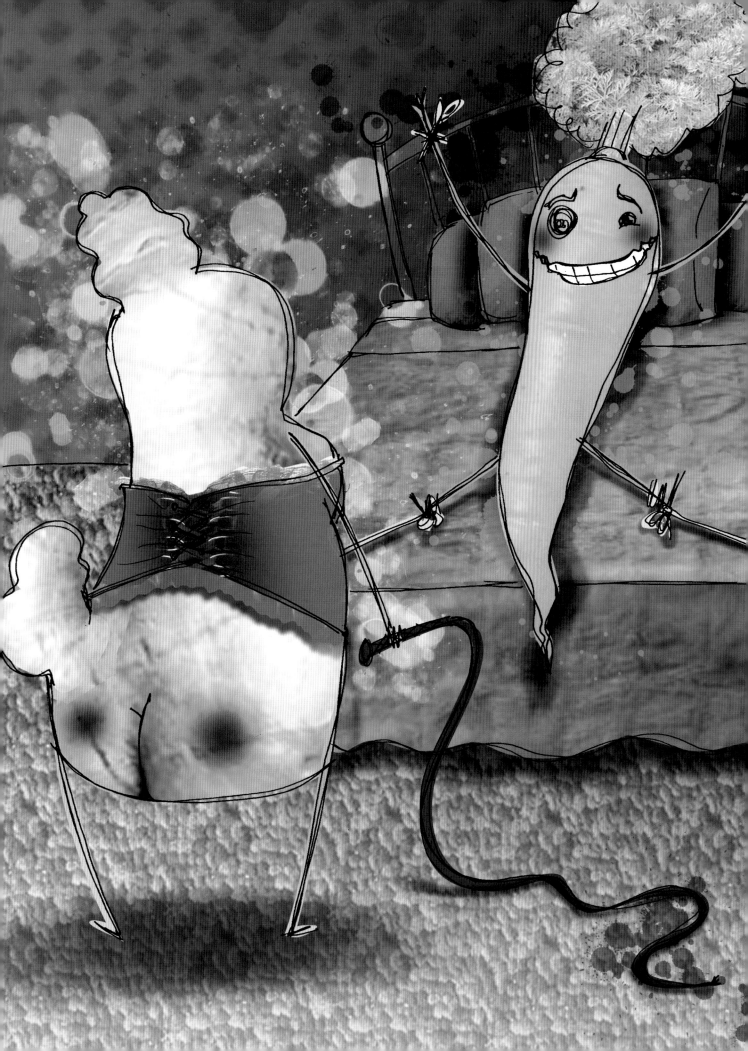

food you eat with a

forkenknife

If you are old enough to be reading this and your mom is still cutting your food into bite-sized pieces, you may as well get your umbilical cord reattached.

There comes a time, even for the most spoon-fed, when you have to wean yourself off your mother's care and start fending for yourself. The sooner you can learn to function with a fork and knife, the sooner you can think about leaving the nest.

However, if your umbilical cord is still attached (or reattached), you may want to consider learning to use a fork and knife to cut it off once and for all.

hot, cross bunny

You called her "Flopsy" (her name is Mopsy, her *sister's* name is Flopsy). Now you have a hot, cross bunny on your hands. This type of thing is very common in France, the land of mistresses, marital rifts, *les affaires de la coeur*. To remedy such a situation, the French invented French toast. The French also invented kissing.

hot, cross bunny french toast

handful of chocolate Easter eggs
½ cup heavy cream, divided
4 hot cross buns
2 large eggs
butter

UNWRAP THE EASTER EGGS, and get them in a small pot with $\frac{1}{4}$ cup of the cream. Simmer on very low heat, stirring occasionally, until the chocolate is melted and the sauce is smooth. Go slow and low or you will be elbow deep with a wire scrubby in burnt-chocolate-pot-bottom nastiness . . . and she will be ticked that you even ruined the chocolate. Take off the heat.

Hot cross buns are generally round; trim off the top and bottom so you will end up with flat slices. The buns can also be rather small, so each one should yield 2 or 3 slices. You be the judge based on how thick you want each piece.

Crack the eggs in a bowl, and whisk them together with the remaining $\frac{1}{4}$ cup of cream. You don't need to add any sugar or flavouring to this recipe because the buns are already sweet and spicy.

They are also pretty soft and squishy—they only need a light coating with the egg goop, with no need to soak them all the way through like you would with plain crusty bread. Preheat a frying pan on medium heat. When it is warm, add butter and let it melt but not brown. Gently lay down the egg-doused buns, and cook until the edges are golden and crispy. You should only flip it once. (Either with a flipper or with just a quick jerk of the pan with your arm. But be honest with yourself. Are you sure you can flip these without a flipper? It's a tricky move that takes practice. So with everything on the line, is this the right time to be risking it?)

When the French toast is ready, arrange it on a plate and drizzle liberally with the chocolate sauce.

CHOC-A-LOT OR
CHOC-A-LITTLE

There is a reverse ratio applied to drizzling chocolate on food: the less chocolate you drizzle the prettier it will look and the less enjoyment you will get from it.

So let the pleasure flow.

lumberjack flapjacks

Perhaps the wood is always best first thing in the morning, because nothing gets lumberjacks up faster than morning wood. But what keeps lumberjacks going all day long? Light, fluffy pancakes, full of hearty energy to keep their axes swinging from morning to night. And if you want to go at it all day like a lumberjack, here are some recipes so you can enjoy pancakes for breakfast, lunch, or dinner.

stack of lumberjack flapjacks

1 cup whole wheat flour

1 tsp baking powder

1 tsp baking soda

pinch of salt

3 eggs

1 cup plain yogurt

butter for the pan

PANCAKE PADDLING

Sure, some lumberjacks love a good paddling on their backsides, but never, ever pat the backside of your pancake. You'll knock out all the air bubbles . . . from the pancake. Remember the one-flip rule: only flip a pancake once—no flipping it back onto the first side. We take pancakes seriously in Canada, and it's considered a felony here to flip pancakes more than once.

PLACE A LARGE non-stick pan on your stovetop set to just below medium . . . not any higher! Let the pan heat up.

Sift all the dry ingredients into a medium bowl. Now separate the eggs into 2 large bowls—the bowl for the egg whites should be scrupulously clean. Beat the egg whites into stiff peaks with a whisk or electric mixer. And to the bowl with the egg yolks, add the yogurt and combine.

Add the dry ingredients to the yolk/yogurt mixture and mix until thoroughly incorporated. Now count to 10 slowly . . . the baking soda needs a few seconds to react with the acidity from the yogurt, making the batter puff up a bit. Now add half the stiff egg whites, and with a rubber spatula gently fold it in until evenly mixed. Finally, fold in the remaining egg whites. Get ready to make some pancakes.

Get a blop of butter onto the hot pan, and put down some batter to form 4-inch pancakes, with plenty of room in between to make flipping easy.

These are thick pancakes. The bubbles won't rise to the top like other pancakes, which is usually a handy sign they're ready to be flipped. Be watchful and flip when the outside bottom edges are golden brown. You'll get the hang of it pretty quickly—just remember, you can only flip a pancake once.

Serve immediately in a big stack with warm maple syrup and soft butter.

MAKES 6 TO 7 LIGHT AND FLUFFY 4-INCH PANCAKES.

BMP: *BACON* AND *MAPLE* SYRUP ON *PANCAKE*

Pack a hearty lunch with your leftover pancakes. Just slap a couple pieces of bacon (the regular kind or Canadian bacon) and a swizzle of maple syrup between two pancakes, and *voilà*, you have a pancake picnic. Also try adding lettuce and tomato and a gloop of mayo for a hearty BLT.

fully stacked buffalo burger

Candy apple onions

2 Tbsp vegetable oil

1 red onion, chopped

1 Granny Smith apple, diced

salt and pepper

1 Tbsp maple syrup

1 tsp apple cider vinegar

Burger

1 ½ lb ground buffalo

vegetable oil for the pan

salt and fresh-cracked pepper

8 oz Monterey Jack, grated

To serve

8 leftover 4-inch pancakes

sliced tomato

leafy green lettuce

mayonnaise

CANDY APPLE ONIONS

The trick to caramelizing onions is to take your time over medium-low heat. This does the best job of caramelizing the sugars. And up the sweetness by adding maple syrup toward the end.

GET A FRYING PAN over medium-low heat. Heat up the oil, toss in the onion, and sweat it slowly until it's soft. Continue cooking to let it develop a little colour and caramelize (this will take about 30 minutes), then add the diced apple, and cook until all the sugars start to get brown and sticky delicious. Season with salt and pepper, stir in the maple syrup and vinegar, and cook for 1 more minute. Transfer the sweet oniony-apple mess to a bowl for easy spooning.

Don't bother mixing spices or breadcrumbs or eggs or any of that stuff into your burgers. Lumberjacks ain't got time to be fussy like that. Just get the ground bison and simply form it into 4 large balls, then flatten them out so they are a bit wider than your pancakes because they will shrink when they cook.

Get a large pan on medium heat, and when it is hot, toss in a glug of oil. When the oil is hot, get the burgers in the pan. Just leave them in one spot so they can cook slowly and get some nice brown colouring—don't muck around with them too much. Flip when the blood beads up on the top.

As soon as you flip the burgers, season them with salt and fresh-cracked pepper and get the cheese on so it will have time to get melty and maybe get a bit of burnt-cheesy-edged goodness. Cook according to your doneness preference.

Warm up your leftover pancakes in the toaster or a 400°F oven for about 5 minutes to get them toasty. Start stacking with a good smear of the candy apple onions on the bottom pancake, top with the burger patty, some lettuce, tomato, and mayonnaise, and another pancake.

Enjoy with your Canadian friends, who will be sure to thank you. No dou't, eh?

MAKES 4 BURGERS.

religious hollandaise

There are a lot of different types of Christians, and they tend to disagree on a surprisingly large number of technicalities. But one thing they would probably all agree on is that it is perfectly acceptable to skip church if you stay home and make eggs Benedict.

The simple act of preparing eggs Benedict will cleanse your soul and instantly absolve you of all your sins. Learn how to make it really well and you can lock down a seat next to The Big Guy.

If you don't believe what I've said so far, ask your cardinal, or pastor or whatever, just to be sure. Just because it's in the book doesn't make it completely true or free from interpretation and whatnot. Same with the following hollandaise commandments . . . but I'd follow them just to be on the safe side.

Hollandaise sauce

3 eggs (you'll be using only the yolks)
1 lemon
½ pound cold butter
pinch of salt

SEPARATE THE EGGS. (You can keep the egg whites for later—for an omelette or meringues or whatever.) Juice the lemon. Cut the cold butter into cubes the size of playing dice.

Put the yolks, lemon juice, butter, and salt into a cold medium-sized pot. Get out your whisk and put the pot over medium heat. Stir—you don't have to stir hard, you don't have to stir quickly, you just have to stir constantly. Don't think you can walk away for a second. Keep going until the butter melts. You'll notice the sauce starting to get smooth and creamy, but not as thick as hollandaise should be. Just be patient and keep stirring. It will start to thicken up.

When it is the nice, rich, and velvety consistency of hollandaise, remove it (and keep it away) from the heat source. Ideally you want to use it immediately, but if that's not possible just make sure it doesn't sit around for more than an hour. If it becomes too thick as it sits, whisk in a couple drops of warm water to loosen it up.

Serve with cooked asparagus, with steak, or on eggs Benedict . . . turn the page for several variations.

THE ELEVEN HOLLANDAISE COMMANDMENTS

1. Thou shalt forget what thou thinkest thou knowest of hollandaise.
2. Thou shalt combine thine ingredients whilst cold.
3. Thou shalt whisk directly in a metal pot with thine metal whisk.
4. Thou shalt whisk slowly and steadily on the stove without stopping so as not to break thine emulsion.
5. Thou shalt maketh sure the heat is medium-low so thine sauce becometh neither too hot nor too cold.
6. Thou shalt remove thine saucepot from thine heat source when thine sauce be velvety thick, lest it become too gloppy.
7. Thou shalt add two drops of warm water whilst whisking shouldst thine sauce become too gloppy.
8. Thou shalt taste thine sauce, and forthwith adjust thine seasoning with salt and lemon juice if it be needed.
9. If thine sauce be broken, thou must start again. To thine new sauce thou mayest drizzle in thine broken sauce whilst whisking with great vigour.
10. Thou shalt not covet thy neighbour's sauce, and thou shalt make thine better.
11. Thou shalt always lick the whisk clean.

the blessed eggs of st. benedictus
traditional eggs benedict

If you want to know the real story, the whole eggs Benedict thing started back in the day with a chicken herder named Ben "Benny" Benedictus. One night, he had a dream about a creamy, delicious sauce to put on his poached eggs. The next morning he woke up, made the first batch of hollandaise sauce for brunch, and suddenly cherubs started strumming and he became an instant saint.

Incidentally, it was his twin brother Owen who created the Benedictine monks.

1 recipe hollandaise sauce (page 95)

8 eggs

2 Tbsp white vinegar (any kind)

10 oz thinly sliced Black Forest ham

4 English muffins split in half

MAKE A BATCH of hollandaise sauce.

To poach the eggs, fill a large pot with about 4 inches of water. You can use holy water if you can get it, but tap water is fine otherwise. Bring the water to a boil and reduce the heat to medium so it maintains a gentle simmer. Add the vinegar.

Meanwhile, heat up the ham in a frying pan on low heat and toast the English muffins.

Poach no more than 4 eggs at a time. Crack an egg into a small bowl without breaking the yolk, dip the bowl on an angle into the water, and gently tip the egg into the water. Repeat with each egg. Try not to poach your fingers.

When the egg is in the water, don't mess around with it—just let the egg white set up. The egg should then float to the surface, but if it doesn't, very gently use a spatula to coax it off the bottom. After about 4 to 5 minutes, when the egg white is firm and there is just a slight jiggle around the yolk, remove the egg from the water with a slotted spoon.

Place 2 toasted English muffin halves on each plate, top each half with some warm ham, and lay your poached egg on the ham. Smother on a generous golden blanket of hollandaise sauce.

Serve with slices of melon or some pan-fried potatoes.

SERVES 4.

the blessed eggs of st. florentino
dirty poached eggs with balsamic spinach

There was a farmer named Firenze Florentino who lived long ago in the "upper shin" of the boot shape that is Italy, in a place we know as Florence. Most of the gardens around there were rock gardens with marble statues and no plants whatsoever. So everyone thought he was crazy when he started growing spinach.

One morning he went to enjoy his eggs Benedict in the garden, but he dropped them on the way in a patch of spinach. He gathered it all up, but back on his plate the eggs were dirty with spinach all over them. Not wanting to waste good food, he just ate it anyways, and—*bing bang boom*—angels appeared and he was suddenly St. Florentino like it ain't no thang.

1 recipe hollandaise sauce (page 95)

8 eggs

1 cup balsamic vinegar (more for the spinach)

olive oil for sautéing the spinach

3 cloves garlic

10 oz fresh baby spinach

2 Tbsp balsamic vinegar

2 Tbsp butter

salt to taste

4 English muffins split in half

MAKE A BATCH of hollandaise sauce.

To poach the eggs, fill a large pot with about 4 inches of water. Bring the water to a boil and reduce the heat to medium so it maintains a gentle simmer. Here's the trick to make the eggs dirty and delicious: add a cup of cheap balsamic vinegar. Return it to a simmer.

For the spinach, get a large pan over medium-high heat. Heat the oil, toss in the whole cloves of garlic, and pile on all the spinach. It may seem like too much spinach, but eventually most of the moisture will be cooked off to make just the right amount. Add the 2 Tbsp balsamic, the butter, and a sprinkling of salt. Let the butter melt, remove the garlic cloves, and keep the spinach warm.

Toast the English muffins.

Poach no more than 4 eggs at a time. Crack an egg into a small bowl without breaking the yolk, dip the bowl on an angle into the water, and gently tip the egg into the water. Repeat with each egg. Try not to poach your fingers.

When the egg is in the water, don't mess around with it—just let the egg white set up. The egg should then float to the surface, but if it doesn't, very gently use a spatula to coax it off the bottom. After about 4 to 5 minutes, when the egg white is firm and there is just a slight jiggle around the yolk, remove the egg from the water with a slotted spoon.

Place 2 toasted English muffin halves on each plate, top each half with some sautéed spinach, and lay your dirty poached egg on the spinach. Smother on a generous golden blanket of hollandaise sauce.

Serve with slices of melon or some pan-fried potatoes.

SERVES 4.

the blessed eggs of ste. anise

eggs benedict with plenty of fennel

When Anise was young she would practise running a marathon to school and back from school every day.

In ancient Greece, the word for fennel was *marathon*. In Anise's world, they commemorate the origins of the word by awarding you fennel for winning a marathon. Since Anise could win a marathon with both legs tied up, she ended up with a lot of fennel.

With metabolism like a racehorse, she ate all the time, and usually something with fennel. So it was inevitable that she would one day make eggs Benedict with fennel bulb and fennel seeds, garnished with fennel fronds, and when she did so a heavenly procession of cherubs raced in to pronounce her a saint.

1 large fennel bulb with fronds

vegetable oil for roasting

salt and fresh-cracked pepper

1 recipe hollandaise sauce (page 95)

2 Tbsp whole fennel seeds

2 Tbsp white vinegar (any kind)

8 eggs

4 English muffins split in half

PREHEAT THE OVEN to 350°F.

First prep your fennel way ahead, as it takes 2½ hours to roast. Cut off the tops of the fennel so you are left with the main bulb, but reserve the tops and pick off the most tender tiny fronds and chop them for mixing into the hollandaise. Trim off the dirty bottom root end. With the bottom facing up, cut the fennel into 8 wedges—each wedge should be held together by the root end. Lay the wedges in a baking dish and drizzle on some oil, then flip them over to drizzle them on the other side. Sprinkle on some salt and pepper. Cover the dish with foil and roast for 2½ hours.

When the fennel is done roasting, you can start the rest of the recipe.

Make a batch of hollandaise sauce.

To poach the eggs, fill a large pot with about 4 inches of water. Add the fennel seeds when the water comes to a boil. Reduce the heat to medium so it maintains a gentle simmer. Add the vinegar.

Toast the English muffins.

Poach no more than 4 eggs at a time. Crack an egg into a small bowl without breaking the yolk, dip the bowl on an angle into the water, and gently tip the egg into the water. Repeat with each egg. Try not to poach your fingers.

When the egg is in the water, don't mess around with it—just let the egg white set up. The egg should then float to the surface, but if it doesn't, very gently use a spatula to coax it off the bottom. After about 4 to 5 minutes, when the egg white is firm and there is just a slight jiggle around the yolk, remove the egg from the water with a slotted spoon.

Place 2 toasted English muffin halves on a plate, and top each half with 1 wedge of fennel fanned out nicely. Lay your poached egg on the fennel. Stir the fennel fronds into the hollandaise at the last minute, and smother on a generous golden blanket of hollandaise sauce.

Serve with slices of melon or some pan-fried potatoes.

SERVES 4.

the blessed eggs of st. tommasso
eggs benedict in purgatory with tomatoes

Tommasso was the chief internal liaison officer for the international public/privacy commission of tomato affairs. In other words, he was a bureaucrat. Through the careful use of public relations and liberal use of paperwork he made sure that people never discovered that tomatoes were actually fruit.

As he was trying to think of more ways to make tomatoes less fruit-like, he had the idea to make tomato eggs Benedict. On the idea alone the cherubs were dispatched, but they were confused when they arrived and there was nothing being served. Luckily Tommasso started talking about typing a report and having some mock-ups made. He kept talking all day without saying anything and finally the cherubs relented and made him a saint anyway.

1 recipe hollandaise sauce (page 95)

8 slices pancetta

2 Tbsp vegetable oil

1 pint cherry tomatoes, halved

salt and pepper

6 cups tomato juice or veg juice

4 English muffins split in half

8 eggs

MAKE A BATCH of hollandaise sauce.

Get a medium pan onto the stove over medium heat and cook the pancetta in oil until it's crispy. Set aside. Use the pancetta fat in the pan to sauté the tomatoes over low heat with a pinch of salt and a crack of pepper.

To poach the eggs, fill a large pot with the tomato juice. Bring it to a boil and reduce the heat to medium so it maintains a gentle simmer. (The tomato juice does not need vinegar.)

Toast the English muffins.

Poach no more than 4 eggs at a time. Crack an egg into a small bowl without breaking the yolk, dip the bowl on an angle into the tomato juice, and gently tip the egg into the juice. Repeat with each egg. Try not to poach your fingers.

You will quickly discover that you have lost the egg in the opacity of the juice.

When the egg is in the juice, don't mess around with it—just let the egg white set up. The egg should then float to the surface, but if it doesn't, very gently use a spatula to coax it off the bottom. After about 4 to 5 minutes, when the egg white is firm and there is just a slight jiggle around the yolk, remove the egg from the liquid with a slotted spoon.

Place 2 toasted English muffin halves on a plate, top each half with some warm sautéed tomatoes and a slice of crispy pancetta, and lay your poached egg on the pancetta. Smother on a generous golden blanket of hollandaise sauce.

Serve with slices of melon or some pan-fried potatoes.

SERVES 4.

the blessed eggs of st. sålmjun
eggs benedict with homemade gravlax

Sålmjun Laxen woke up every morning to go fishing. Then he would go home and eat salmon gravlax for breakfast. He ate gravlax on everything, from bagels to omelettes. But the day he put it on eggs Benedict he reeled some cherubs hook, line, and sinker . . . and Sålmjun became a saint.

Gravlax

½ cup sugar

¼ cup kosher salt

1 lb fillet of very fresh salmon, with skin

1 bunch of fresh dill, chopped (reserve some for garnish)

Eggs Benedict

1 recipe hollandaise sauce (page 95)

8 eggs

2 Tbsp white vinegar (any kind)

4 English muffins split in half

½ red onion, chopped

20 capers

GRAVLAX VS. SMOKED SALMON

If you give a man some smoked-salmon eggs Benedict you will feed him for a day. Teach a man to make his own gravlax and you won't have to share your fish with him again.

Gravlax and smoked salmon are the result of different methods of cold curing, which helps preserve the fish plus enhance texture and flavour. Smoked salmon uses cold smoke, while gravlax uses only salt and sugar. Smoking your own salmon is complicated, but you can easily make your own gravlax in the comfort of your kitchen.

Freshness is key to this preparation. Frozen fish is not an acceptable alternative.

YOU WILL HAVE to make the gravlax at least 24 hours ahead.

Mix the sugar and salt together—this will be your curing mix. Prepare your salmon by removing the bones, but keep the skin on. Slice the salmon into 2 equal pieces. Get a big piece of plastic wrap on the counter and sprinkle on an even layer of the sugar-salt mix the size of the salmon fillet. Place 1 fillet skin side down on the curing mix. Sprinkle on curing mix to cover the top and sides of the salmon. Lay down an even layer of dill, more curing mix, and top it with the other piece of salmon, skin side up. Cover the top and sides with the remaining curing mix. It should look a bit like a dill sandwich on salmon bread that fell in the sand.

Use your super-strength to tightly wrap the salmon stack. Use another piece of plastic wrap to wrap it even tighter. Then wrap it in foil, place it on a plate with a weighted tray on top, and stuff it in your fridge.

After 24 hours in the fridge, unwrap it, remove the excess dill, and pat the salmon dry with a paper towel. Use a super-sharp knife to slice off thin sheets of salmon on an angle, like smoked salmon.

Make a batch of hollandaise sauce.

To poach the eggs, fill a large pot with about 4 inches of water. Bring the water to a boil and reduce the heat to medium so it maintains a gentle simmer. Add the vinegar.

Toast the English muffins.

Poach no more than 4 eggs at a time. Crack an egg into a small bowl without breaking the yolk, dip the bowl on an angle into the water, and gently tip the egg into the water. Repeat with each egg. Try not to poach your fingers.

When the egg is in the water, don't mess around with it—just let the egg white set up. The egg should then float to the surface, but if it doesn't, very gently use a spatula to coax it off the bottom. After about 4 to 5 minutes, when the egg white is firm and there is just a slight jiggle around the yolk, remove the egg from the water with a slotted spoon.

Place 2 toasted English muffin halves on a plate, and top each half with a lovely pile of sliced gravlax. Lay down a poached egg, and smother on a generous golden blanket of hollandaise sauce. Top with red onion, capers, and some of the leftover fresh dill.

Serve with slices of melon or some pan-fried potatoes.

SERVES 4. ANY LEFTOVER GRAVLAX WILL BE DELICIOUS ON A BAGEL WITH CREAM CHEESE, RED ONIONS, AND CAPERS.

single served

Okay, so, a guy takes his shopping basket to the cute girl's checkout. From his basket he takes one apple, one can of chili, one chocolate bar, one frozen dinner, one litre of milk, etc.

The checkout girl looks at him and at all his purchases and says, "You must be single."

The guy blushingly replies, "Yeah, how did you know?"

The girl shrugs and says, "Because you're ugly."

single lasagna

If you are a single guy or gal, you need to know how to make single lasagna. It does double duty of being a great, easy meal to make for yourself and, if you do end up landing a first date, ensuring you don't stay single for long.

FILLER

Pick and choose from the following, and if you have any other ideas, make sure they are ingredients that don't require cooking and just require a heating through. So if you are using chicken, cook it first instead of adding it in raw.

- fresh basil leaves
- fresh arugula or spinach
- sautéed mushrooms
- marinated artichoke hearts, diced
- marinated spicy eggplant
- pan-fried zucchini
- fresh grape tomatoes, halved
- roasted garlic (page 73)
- olives (pitted or stuffed)
- caramelized onions
- toasted pine nuts
- anchovies (seriously, yum)
- canned tuna, drained and chunked
- prosciutto
- cooked bacon, chopped
- cooked ground meat
- chorizo

FRESH PASTA SHEETS

Fresh pasta sheets are the lynchpin of this dish. Little Italian shops usually stock them, or you can order ahead if your shop sells out quickly. Dried pasta won't work for this recipe, and the fresh stuff is only a little bit more coin and totally worth it. Cut the sheets into approximately 6-inch squares, or whatever size your ovenproof serving dishes are.

CHEESE

The best is sliced bocconcini (little baby mozzarellas), but you can use any kind of mozzarella, as long as it is soft, white, and not a gnarly rubber nugget. Try a little Parmesan or Asiago for the top of the lasagna to give it some brown crusty goodness.

SAUCE

Pick your favourite tomato sauce or Alfredo sauce recipe, or any of the pestos on page 113.

PREHEAT THE OVEN to 350°F.

Bloop a little sauce into 1 (or 2 if you are blooping for 2) ceramic, ovenproof serving dish(es) (this can be a plate as long as there is a little lip), enough so the first sheet of pasta doesn't touch and thereby stick to the bottom.

On top of the first sheet of pasta, place your fillers of choice. Drizzle on some more sauce and sprinkle on some grated mozza. Do a second layer: pasta, toppings, sauce, cheese. Finish with a layer of pasta topped with sauce, mozza, a little Parm, and a drizzle of good olive oil. Don't worry about stuff leaking out and it not looking perfect. It will still taste awesome. Beauty is in the eye of the beholder.

Blap it in the oven for approximately 20 minutes (or more, based on how thick you layered it all). You are looking for golden brown bubbly goodness on the cheese to know it is done.

Eat this directly from the serving dish (use a placemat on your dining table), with some mixed greens on the side.

GET SOME SATISFACTION
You (and hopefully your date) will be thoroughly impressed by the lasagna. Although it may be time to do something about the single-signature milk-crate furniture.

pesto change-o

Here is a great trick to have up your sleeve. Pick a bunch of leafy herbs or fragrant greens, some nuts, and a binding liquid, and like magic you can make a variety of pestos that will, again like magic, transform pasta, grilled meat or fish, and even seasonal fruit into something spellbinding. Here are some great combinations to try.

old magic, new magic

Traditionally pestos are made using a mortar and pestle. A mortar is a large heavy bowl carved from marble, but it can also be made from ceramic or cast iron. The pestle is a mashing device made of the same material as the bowl and used to pulverize the contents of the bowl. The words "pesto" and "pestle" derive from the same Latin root word that means to pound or crush.

To make any of these pestos, combine all the ingredients in a mortar and pestle. To make larger batches in a fraction of the time, try using your whiz-bang blender.

Freeze the leftovers in ice-cube trays covered in cling wrap for handy pesto hits whenever you need them. No matter how much pesto you freeze for another day, it has a tendency to disappear . . . kinda like magic!

lemony pesto

YOU CAN SERVE this pesto with pasta. Or with simply prepared salmon as a condiment or slathered on top for last two minutes of cooking. The meal is complete with boiled potatoes and green beans.

1 bunch fresh parsley

a large handful of arugula

1 clove garlic, grated or finely minced

1 cup walnuts

zest and juice of 1 lemon

salt to taste

½ cup walnut or canola oil

cilantro pesto

SIMPLY GRILL A piece of chicken, slice it into bite-sized pieces, and douse it in cilantro pesto. Serve it with coconut rice and some fresh bean sprouts in a bowl with chopsticks and lime wedges. Or bake fish with the pesto on top as above.

1 cup tightly packed fresh cilantro leaves

¼ cup roasted salted peanuts

3 Tbsp rice wine vinegar or lime juice

a couple drops sesame oil

a bit of fresh red or green chili, minced

¼ cup canola oil

minty pesto

HAZELNUTS HAVE A beautiful fragrance, but are difficult to pulverize because they are so hard. Almonds are also a little tough. Both nuts will benefit from a quick toasting to make them easier to chop-chop and to enhance their flavour. Get almonds and hazelnuts without skin, which adds an unfavourable texture and colour. Serve on strawberries, melon, or oranges.

4 cups packed fresh mint leaves

1 cup toasted, blanched almonds or hazelnuts

½ cup honey

½ cup walnut or canola oil

dr. frankensteinmanburg

Oy vey! Trying to please your mother can be enough to drive any scientist mad. Revolutionize reanimation technology and your mother accuses you of playing God.

   "It isn't a game! Why don't you meet a nice girl instead of spending all your time with the potatoes and the squashes and the bits and pieces and the large latke monster? *Oy!* Everyone says you used to be such a nice, bright young man! Ah, but what can I do . . ."

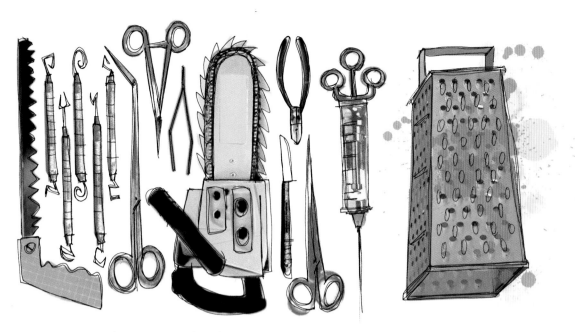

mix and match latkes bits and pieces

Mixing and matching is all part of the fun. So pick two or three (or more) of these roots and tubers to make your own custom monster-latke creations. For the best results, stick with potatoes as the main component and add from there.

AIR ON THE SIDE OF CAUTION

To prevent your shredded flesh from discolouring from oxidation, the only real trick is to work quickly. However, if the shredded flesh does turn brown, rest assured this will have little effect on the flavour and will only affect the look. When you're building a monster, why worry about aesthetics?

POTATO
• use potatoes as the main ingredient for latkes
• binds latkes nicely; starchy potatoes (like russets) are especially good
• after grating, squeeze out excess liquid
• oxidizes to a brown (see sidebar)

SWEET POTATO
• its natural sugars can burn quickly
• benefits from slow cooking
• great sweet earthy flavour
• oxidizes to a brown

YAM
• its natural sugars can burn quickly
• benefits from slow cooking
• great sweet flavour
• oxidizes to a greenish brown

CELERIAC
• awesome flavour
• poor binder, needs extra flour
• oxidizes to a greenish brown

PARSNIP
• great flavour
• use only a small amount
• poor binder, needs extra flour
• does not oxidize

PUMPKIN
• amazingly light texture
• fantastic flavour
• moderate binder, needs extra flour
• no oxidizing, great colour

BUTTERNUT SQUASH
• its natural sugars can burn quickly
• phenomenal flavour
• moderate binder, needs extra flour
• no oxidizing, great colour

dr. frankensteinmanburg's latkes

It's much harder to find slightly used human body parts than it is to find roots and squashes. So have fun mixing and matching these squashes, tubers, and roots to make your own formula for latkes. Sure you'll still have people breaking down your door, but at least instead of pitchforks and torches they'll just be carrying regular forks and an appetite.

2 cups (or more) shredded
    vegetable flesh
2 Tbsp flour (for every 2 cups flesh)
1 egg (for every 2 cups flesh)
salt
vegetable oil for the pan
butter
sour cream
applesauce (store-bought or
    homemade; recipe follows)

AFTER YOU PEEL and grate your assorted squashes, roots, and tubers, you will need to measure them out to know how much flour, egg, and salt to use. For every 2 cups of vegetable flesh add the called-for amount of flour and egg and a pinch of salt.

Make sure to squeeze out the excess liquid from the potatoes before adding to the mixing bowl. Mix all ingredients thoroughly with your hand.

Get a large frying pan onto medium-low heat. You want to keep the temperature nice and low for slow browning and even cooking. Heat 2 Tbsp oil.

Make 4 small haystack-like mounds in the pan at a time, with plenty of space between each. Use a flipper to flatten the stacks down hard until they are ½ inch thick. Cook until brown and golden on the underside, then flip and continue cooking until brown on the other side. When they are almost finished, add 1 Tbsp butter to the pan to melt and make the latkes glossy. Continue with the rest of the grated flesh.

Serve with a scoop of sour cream and applesauce.

TWO CUPS OF SHREDDED VEGETABLE FLESH MAKES ENOUGH LATKES FOR 2 RAVENOUS VILLAGERS.

gratest applesauce

While you're grating things, grab a few apples and rake 'em over the grater to make a quick applesauce.

4 apples (Granny Smith is good)
juice of 1 lemon
1 Tbsp sugar
pinch salt
½ cup water

PEEL, CORE, AND grate the apples directly into a medium-sized pot. Add all the other ingredients, and get the pot on low heat until the apples get tender and soft and the whole mess turns into a lovely sweet and tart applesauce. This should take about 30 minutes or so.

equal roots movement

The underground movement is about to surface. No longer will the root-vegetable minority be kept down by oppressive carrots and potatoes. With so many roots being ignorantly ignored, it is important to know you have alternatives.

Open your heart and your mouth, and join the uprising of the turnip, rutabaga, and parsnip. Enjoy the new root order with remakes of those classic recipes written for the oppressor root.

rutabaga anna

Rutabagas have taken a pounding from potatoes. But pound for pound, rutabagas are way more interesting than potatoes when it comes to mashing, puréeing, and especially slow-roasting—like in this recipe. Rutabagas are not just bigger and cheaper than potatoes, they also taste a helluva lot better in this classic layered potato dish.

4 large rutabagas
½ cup butter, melted
fresh thyme leaves
salt and pepper

PREHEAT THE OVEN to 300°F.

Trim the tops and bottoms of the rutabagas. Trim the sides to form a cylinder or can shape, with the top and bottom being the flat ends of the can. If that means trimming a lot off the sides, don't sweat it. Rutabagas are dirt cheap, and this will make slicing so much easier.

Make thin disc-shaped slices ⅛ inch thick, either with a mandoline or with a knife. If you're doing it with a knife, make sure it is sharp and you know how to use it.

Butter up a large round baking dish or deep pie plate, and carefully arrange your first layer of rutabaga, starting from the outside in a circular pattern and overlapping the discs until you reach the middle.

Evenly drizzle some melted butter on the first layer. Sprinkle with the thyme and salt and pepper.

Add another layer of rutabaga, then more butter, thyme, salt, and pepper. Continue layering, and finish your last layer with a drizzle of butter. Top with a piece of parchment paper cut to fit.

If you have a pan the same size or slightly smaller, fill it with water and carefully put it on top to weigh down the rutabagas. A heavy lid would work too.

Blap it in the oven for about 3 to 4 hours. It's very forgiving if you leave it in longer.

When the rutabagas are soft and the edges develop some nice brown colour, remove them from the oven and allow them to cool for at least 30 minutes with the weight still on top.

Remove the weight (or the lid) and the parchment, and put your cutting board or serving dish upside down right on the pan. Hold both of them firmly together on the sides, and flip it over quickly. Think about it before you try it so you get the idea of how it's going to work, or else you will have made "Rutabaga Pile-of-Mess." Remove the pan and marvel at the beauty.

CUT LIKE A PIE AND SERVE TO THE 5 NEWEST MEMBERS OF THE RUTABAGA FAN CLUB. THIS DISH GETS ALONG WITH ROAST PORK OR BEEF AND RED WINE.

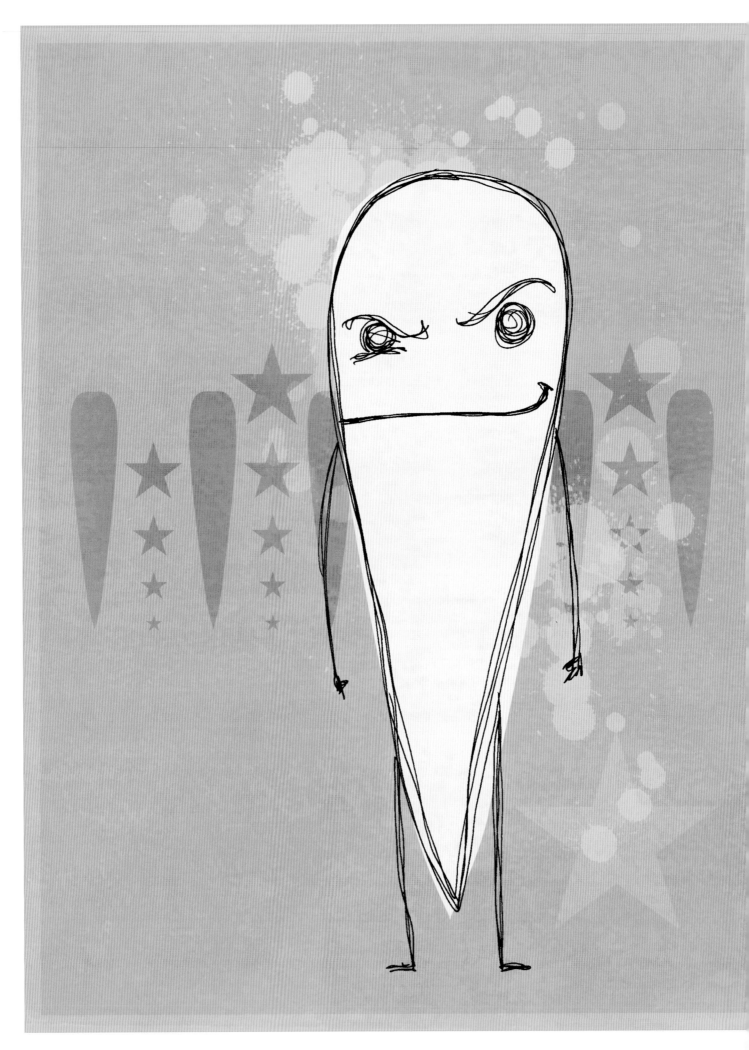

parsnip and ginger, the hot new soupness

Carrots are so full of themselves. They are tall and fancy looking, and you find them at la-dee-da-dee parties, often flirting. Which may explain why carrots have managed to hook up with a sexy spice like ginger. But instead of hanging around with such a conceited root, ginger would be much better off with the modest parsnip.

It is just as tall, but the carrot's pale and less attractive cousin is always getting overlooked. For those who know how sweet and complex parsnip can be, it is hard to ever imagine going back. Sure, the carrot has more mass appeal, but in the right circumstances parsnips can be so much more fulfilling.

5 small parsnips
salt for boiling the parsnips
a big honking chunk of ginger
1 cup heavy cream
1 Tbsp white wine vinegar
fresh-cracked pepper
chopped fresh chives

PEEL AND ROUGHLY chop the parsnips into ½-inch rounds. Place the parsnips into a pot, and add enough cold water to cover by about 2 inches.

Bring to a boil and add salt.

In the meantime, grate your ginger to a fine pulpy mush into a small bowl. You don't have to worry about peeling it first.

When the water boils, reduce the heat to medium to avoid the pot boiling over, and let it bubble away until the parsnips are soft and just starting to fall apart at the edges. It's better to overcook than to undercook the parsnips.

Turn off the heat, remove from the hot burner, and let it cool down for 5 minutes. Carefully pour all of it into a blender.

Again, be very careful. You need to blend it while it is hot to make it smooth, but you also have to be careful not to blast molten lava parsnips all over your kitchen and vital body parts. Remove the little plastic thingy from the blender lid, and cover the hole with a tea towel. (This stops it from being airtight, which would cause an ugly kick at the start—although the steam can sometimes get hot on your hand.) Start on low, and build up the speed incrementally.

When the soup is looking smooth, turn it off and pour in the cream and ginger. Put the lid and tea towel back on and blend it some more.

Carefully pour the soup back into the pot, and starting on low heat, increase the heat to medium—gradually, or the soup will start sputtering all over the place like it is about to erupt, and your house will look like Pompeii.

Add the vinegar right before serving, and then pour the soup into bowls. Garnish with fresh-cracked pepper and nicely chopped chives for prettiness.

IMPRESS YOU AND 5 FRIENDS AT YOUR LA-DEE-DA-DEE PARSNIP PARTY.

turnip the champ

Ireland has strong traditions when it comes to potatoes and to fighting. Traditional Irish Champ is made with mashed potatoes, spring onions, and butter. So when you introduce a dish that takes the potato out of a national Irish dish, there's going to be some fisticuffs. But turnip, the great white hope, is poised to knock out the spud and take the belt as the new reigning champ.

Spring onions are traditional, but green onions are more available. Spring onions have a larger bulb and rounder shoots; green onions are smaller and tighter all around.

6 turnips

salt for boiling the turnips

2 spring onions or 4 green onions

¼ cup unsalted butter, divided

salt and pepper

PEEL THE TURNIPS, cut them in half, and place in a pot. Cover with plenty of cold water and lots of salt (enough to make the water taste like the ocean). Bring the water to a rapid boil over high heat, and boil until the turnips turn tender.

While they boil, thinly slice the spring or green onions crosswise, all the way from white to green.

Drain the turnips in a colander, and transfer back into the pot. Mash immediately, and add half the butter and all the white and half the green parts of the onion, mixing it in evenly. Season with salt and pepper to taste.

Scoop them into a big bowl or directly onto individual plates. On each plate, make a small well in the top of each pile. Plop a bit o' butter into each well, and allow it to melt before gobbling. Top with the remaining spring or green onion for garnish.

SERVES 4 AND GETS ALONG WELL WITH SALMON AND LEMON JUICE.

best of the breast

Who else is sick and tired of big, fake breasts?

Those fake chicken breasts are pumped full of enlargement hormones and tightly packaged into vacuum-packed see-thru containers, looking like they are going to burst out at any second. They may be uniform, plump, and perky, but they are certainly not in good taste.

Forget about the double-D chickens and get your hands on some free-range, natural chicken breasts. Sure, free-range breasts are smaller, but they're real, and they're spectacular!

aphrodite's hot greek goddess salad

Aphrodite is the Greek goddess of sexy-time hotness. Besides being the object of everyone's affections, she also has assorted objects of her own to play with. Although she was married to boring old Hephaestus, the hunchback god of blacksmiths, she was often spotted getting around with Aries the macho god of war and Adonis the god of hunkiness.

Variety is the spice of life, and when you are immortal, life needs a lot of variety. This switch-up of the classic Greek salad will heat things up and add some variety to your pleasure palate.

2 free-range chicken breasts,
  preferably boneless, skin-on

Marinade

zest and juice of 1 lemon

2 cloves garlic, crushed

1 tsp oregano

1 tsp salt

crank of pepper

¼ cup olive oil

Dressing

zest and juice of 1 lemon

1 tsp dried oregano

1 tsp salt

crank of pepper

2 Tbsp olive oil

Salad

1 cucumber

2 tomatoes

1 red onion

1 red pepper

To finish

½ cup Greek yogurt

10 pitted kalamata olives

4 oz feta

small bunch fresh parsley
  (preferably flat-leaf), chopped

small bunch dill, chopped

lemon wedges

PREHEAT THE OVEN to 400°F.

Mix all the ingredients for the marinade in a large bowl or baking dish, and make the dressing too while you're at it. Toss the chicken breasts in the marinade to coat, and pop it in the refrigerator until you're ready to cook.

Now chop the cucumber, tomatoes, onion, and red pepper into large chunks, and toss them with the dressing in a large baking dish. Roast for 20 minutes. Remove and stir it all up to move everything around. Remove the chicken breasts from the marinade and place on top of the vegetables with the skin side up. Get the whole thing back in the oven. After 15 minutes, switch the oven to broil, and bake for another 10 minutes, or until the chicken is done and the skin is brown.

Remove the chicken from the dish to let it rest on a plate while you finish the hot Greek salad. Move the veggies to a bowl using a slotted spoon, leaving behind as much of the excess liquid as possible. Mix the yogurt, olives, half the feta, and the freshly chopped parsley and dill with the veggies.

Slice the chicken breasts. Serve an unctuous scoop of roasted salad with the sliced chicken on top. Sprinkle the rest of the feta on top and garnish with lemon wedges.

SERVES 1 RAVENOUS WOMAN AND HER LOVER.

durga's curry

The Hindu goddess Durga somehow manages to keep her strong feminine qualities while still fighting demons. She packs a serious punch with ten super-buff arms and keeps things action-packed with her arsenal of weapons, riding in on her golden lion and swinging a mace, trident, long sword, lotus, conch, bow and arrows, a thunderbolt, and a spinning disc of light. Hell, yeah! No wonder she's a demon slayer.

Included here is a ten-spice curry paste to mix up and keep handy for when you need to slay your hunger demon.

Curry paste

¼ cup whole cumin seeds

1 Tbsp fenugreek seeds

1 Tbsp ground turmeric

2 tsp black peppercorns

1 tsp cayenne pepper

1 tsp fennel seeds

1 tsp whole coriander seeds

1 tsp ground ginger

3 green cardamom pods, husks removed

3 whole cloves

¼ cup vegetable oil (not olive oil)

Chicken

2 free-range chicken breasts, skin on, preferably boneless

vegetable oil for the pan

1 white onion, chopped

1 turnip, cut in ½-inch dice

2 cloves garlic, minced

1 regular can (14 oz) coconut milk

Tart apple relish

1 Granny Smith apple

juice of ½ lemon

1 sprig of fresh cilantro, chopped

salt

FOR THE CURRY PASTE:

Combine all the spices together in a spice grinder, coffee grinder, or a mortar and pestle, and pulverize to a fine powder. Pass the powder through a sieve to remove any big bits of spice that did not get ground up. Mix it with the oil to form a paste.

Keep the curry paste in an airtight container in the fridge for up to a month. The oil will preserve it nicely.

(This makes about 3/4 cup.)

FOR THE CHICKEN CURRY:

Rub the chicken all over with 3 Tbsp of the curry paste.

Now get some oil in a large frying pan, and start to sweat your onion, turnip, and garlic on medium-low heat until the onions are translucent. Clear a spot in the middle of the pan and lay the chicken skin side down right against the frying pan. Cook the chicken slowly, still on medium-low heat, until the skin gets slowly but beautifully crispy. Remove the chicken from the pan (even if it's not completely done yet), and pour in the coconut milk with the onion and turnip, stirring to incorporate. Place the chicken back in the pan with the skin facing up and out of the sauce so it stays crispy. When you think the chicken is cooked through, check that it is no longer pink by removing it from the pan, flipping it over, and then cutting into the thickest part. Cooking times will vary, anywhere from 10 to 15 minutes.

While the chicken cooks, peel, core, and dice the apple and mix in a bowl with the lemon juice, cilantro, and a pinch of salt. Set aside until ready to serve.

Remove the chicken breasts and set aside to rest a bit before slicing. Check the sauce for seasoning and add salt and/or more curry paste if you think it needs some.

Serve the sliced chicken in a little pool of saucy veggies, with steamed basmati rice and a scoop of the tart apple relish.

SERVES 2. MAKE EXTRA IF YOU HAVE A GOLDEN LION FOR A PET.

jeanne's cordon bleu

Jeanne d'Arc was not your typical teenage girl. She didn't have a cell phone, but she *did* have a direct line to The Capital G. So when this French peasant girl claimed that God told her to drive the English out of France and she made some remarkable military predictions, the demoralized French army had no choice but to let her keep talking. She rode out to the front of the French army in a hand-me-down, mix-and-match knight's armour of all white, and against all odds, she kicked some British ass.

However, she was eventually captured by England, deemed a heretic, and burned. Of course there was some rational thinking after the fact, and they were able to get the verdict switched to saint instead of heretic, and she was pronounced a martyr.

Knights of outstanding merit would earn themselves a blue ribbon, or *cordon bleu*. Here's a twist on chicken cordon bleu, usually rolled with the stuffing inside—this one is much easier to assemble. The recipe is dedicated to the late, great Jeanne d'Arc.

3 Tbsp butter

½ cup dry breadcrumbs

pinch of salt for the breadcrumbs

1 cup grated Emmenthal

¼ cup Dijon mustard

4 slices Black Forest ham

2 free-range chicken breasts, skin on, preferably boneless

salt and pepper

2 Tbsp vegetable oil

PREHEAT THE OVEN to broil. Arrange one of the racks nice and low in the oven, pretty far from the element.

Get a small pan and melt the butter over medium heat. Sprinkle in the breadcrumbs. Stir frequently, giving them some time to soak up the butter and start to get brown. Keep a close eye as they can burn easily. Sprinkle in some salt to taste. They are ready when they are golden brown and crunchy. Set aside.

Meanwhile, start grating the cheese, get the mustard in a small bowl, and get your ham ready to go. Pat the chicken dry, and season with salt and pepper.

Get a large ovenproof frying pan (all metal, no plastic) on the stove over medium heat. Heat the oil, and place the chicken skin side down. You're going to flip-flop this chicken a couple times. Cook the chicken breasts for 8 to 10 minutes, until the skin gets crispy and golden. Flip the chicken breasts over so the skin is up, and carefully peel off the skin and set aside on a clean plate. After 5 minutes, flip the chicken so the side previously with the skin is now facing down again. Immediately plop half of the Dijon on each breast and smear to cover, carefully align some ham on top, and liberally sprinkle on the grated cheese. Place the chicken skin jauntily atop the cheese and transfer the whole pan into the oven.

Broil for 5 to 7 minutes, until the skin is crispy and the cheese is a bubbly golden brown. Check to see that the chicken is done by slicing into the thickest part. Let it settle for 5 minutes.

Sprinkle breadcrumbs generously on top for extra crunch. Serve beside boiled potatoes and sautéed green beans.

SERVES 2 FRENCH CHEVALIERS . . . BUT NONE FOR THE BRITISH.

vampire slayer's garlic-laced chicken

When it comes to handling vampire chickens, it isn't enough to just chop off their heads . . . they'll just keep running around. Well, a headless vampire chicken isn't much of a threat considering the fangs are in the beak, but they can still make a big mess with the feathers and blood squirting all over.

The only way to deal with it is to pump it full of garlic, which happens to be a very delicious way of preparing any kind of fowl night creature. Variations on the popular recipe "Chicken with 40 Cloves of Garlic" are actually excellent ways to deal with any kind of poultry, and will help keep all varieties of vampires away.

6 heads of garlic, a glug of olive oil,
   and salt for roasting
2 free-range chicken breasts,
   skin on
salt and pepper to season the
   chicken
1 tsp vegetable oil
1 Tbsp butter
1 shallot, minced
1 glass of white wine
½ cup heavy cream
salt and pepper for the sauce
small handful of parsley, finely
   chopped
sprig of tarragon, leaves only, finely
   chopped

PREHEAT THE OVEN to 400°F.

To roast the garlic, see page 73. Roasting this many heads will take a bit longer, about an hour. Set aside to cool while you prepare the chicken.

Pat the chicken dry with a paper towel and season with salt and pepper.

Get a large ovenproof frying pan (all metal, no plastic) over medium heat. When the pan is hot, dribble in the oil, place the chicken breasts skin side down, and just leave them to let the skin get golden and crispy, about 8 to 10 minutes.

Flip the chicken and immediately transfer the pan to the oven to roast for 10 to 15 minutes, or until the chicken is cooked through.

Prep the rest of the ingredients, which are for the sauce, including squeezing out all the cloves of roasted garlic into a bowl and picking out the stray bits of papery garlic skin.

When the chicken is done, remove the pan from the oven and transfer the chicken to a plate to rest. Using an oven mitt, get the pan back on the stove over high heat to start making the sauce. (Be careful as the handle will stay hot for a long time.) Add the butter to the residual chicken fat and quickly sweat the shallot until translucent.

Add the white wine and cook until the boozy smell evaporates. Add the roasted garlic and roughly mush with a fork to incorporate it with the sauce. Pour in the heavy cream, along with juices from the plate where the chicken is resting, and reduce to thicken the sauce. Remove it from the heat, adjust the flavour with salt and pepper to taste, and finish by mixing in the herbs right before you spoon it generously over the plated chicken.

Serve with big chunks of baguette to sop up the sloppy sauce, or simple boiled potatoes.

WILL SLAY THE HUNGER OF 2 HUNGRY SLAYERS.

the bird and the turd

a cautionary tale

Once upon a time there was a little bird who was a big jerk. Not only did he call the other birds fowl names, he told them that flying south was a stupid idea. They were more than happy to leave without him.

The little bird was overjoyed to be on his own. But he had never been in the north for the winter, so he was unprepared when a snowstorm hit, blew him from his nest, and deposited him into a snowbank two miles down the road.

All he could do was shiver and wait to die.

When a cow spotted the shivering bird, she wanted to help the poor thing. She turned around, lifted her tail, and dropped a hot steamy pile of relief right on top of the bird's head.

The moment it dawned on the bird that he was covered in cow plop, he jumped up and let out a torrent of sailor-calibre slurs. The poor cow, who was only trying to help, decided to walk away, but the bird kept on fiercely cussing.

A curious cat came along to see what all the flapping was about.

The turd-head bird told the cat his sad story. The cat seemed sympathetic and offered to help. He took the little yapper back to the farmhouse and rinsed him clean in a warm soapy bird bath . . . before promptly gobbling him down.

MORALS OF THE STORY

1. Someone who craps on you doesn't necessarily mean you any harm.
2. Someone who hauls you out of crap isn't necessarily looking out for your best interests.
3. Just because someone gives you a recipe that looks like a pile of crap on a plate, it doesn't necessarily mean it's going to taste like crap. Take the next recipe, for example . . .

CRUSTY TOPPER

It may be crustless on the bottom, but you can still call it a pie. Making puff pastry from scratch is a lot of work and it takes some practice . . . so I like to skip all that and just get the frozen stuff. Nothing to feel guilty about. It bakes up nicely and makes a great topper for this pie.

steak and kidney cowpie

1 calf's kidney, or substitute with
    30 button mushrooms, quartered

2 Tbsp white vinegar (any kind)

2 Tbsp kosher or sea salt

2 lb stewing beef or chuck steak,
    cut into 1-inch cubes

vegetable oil for the pan, up to
    2 Tbsp for the onion

1 onion, chopped

3 Tbsp flour

2 cups beef broth

1 cup Guinness

1 Tbsp Worcestershire sauce

pinch of nutmeg

salt and pepper

1 package frozen puff pastry,
    defrosted (read the instructions—
    some take about 2 hours to
    defrost)

SOAK THE KIDNEY overnight in water with the vinegar and salt in the fridge. Replace the soaking solution as often as you like.

Remove and discard the white membranous material from the kidney, dice the glumpy lumps into small $1/2$-inch cubes, and get them into a bowl.

In a big pot over medium-high heat, heat some oil and start to brown the cubed beef in small batches, removing the beef when it is browned onto a large plate or casserole dish. The meat doesn't need to be cooked through, just browned on the outside for flavour. After you have browned all the beef, brown little batches of the kidney (or mushrooms), and then transfer to the same dish as the beef.

Reduce the heat to medium, pour in some oil if the drippings don't amount to about 2 Tbsp, and cook the onion until it is translucent, about 5 minutes. Sprinkle in the flour evenly and mix it up a bit with a wooden spoon. Crank the heat to full blast and throw in the beef broth and the Guinness. Scrape the sticky bits off the bottom of the pan. Now add all the previously browned beef along with its juices, and the kidneys (or mushrooms), Worcestershire sauce, nutmeg, and salt and pepper. Drop the heat to low, cover, and simmer for at least 2 hours.

In the meantime, roll out the puff pastry to $1/2$ inch thick. Using a round cookie cutter, cut out at least 6 rounds of dough, and bake them according to the package's instructions, timing it to be done when you are ready to serve.

To serve, ladle out the pie "filling" into shallow bowls and top with a piece of flaky fresh-from-the-oven puff pastry.

It's as easy as pie . . . actually, it's easier.

SERVES 6 CLOSE FRIENDS WHO DECIDE NOT TO GO SOUTH FOR THE WINTER.

THE OFFAL TRUTH

The biological function of a kidney is to filter urine. The unfortunate result is that kidneys can smell like pee. If you can get over this inevitable truth there are a couple tricks to diminish this smell, like soaking them in vinegar and salt, but the smell will probably linger like your six-year-old cousin's mattress.

If there is absolutely no way you will eat kidney, you can substitute with mushrooms.

suzette's massacre

Here is a grim fairytale about two bloodthirsty psycho killers, one of them a pyromaniac.

Suzette lived alone with her father, Jacques, a poor widowed cobbler in the moderately sized and well-rounded town of Orange.

Suzette would always remember the locket her mother wore containing a photo of Suzette on one side and Jacques on the other. Her mother was wearing it the night she had gone missing while making a late-night shoe delivery. Suzette's mother was not the only mysterious disappearance. Other villagers had also disappeared when wandering alone at night.

The Duke d'Orange ruled this moderately sized town with an iron fist, and was rumoured to have an unnatural bloodlust. It was widely believed he was behind all the mysterious disappearances. However, he had such tremendous influence and power that no one would dare accuse him of such a crime.

One night Suzette's father caught a fever. She realized the baker's clogs would have to be delivered or else there would be no bread. Her father was too weak to object, and so she dashed down the dark streets to the bakery but was struck from behind and knocked unconscious.

Suzette woke up in a great hall full of ornate decorations. When she saw her mother's locket on a side table, she knew the duke was behind her mother's slaying and the murder of all the other missing villagers. She also knew that she would be the next victim of the duke's bloodlust.

The next morning the servants would awaken to find a gruesome scene . . .

suzette's massacre

3 eggs

2 Tbsp sugar (more for the oranges)

pinch of salt

2 cups milk

½ cup cold water

2 cups flour

¼ cup melted butter for the crêpe
    batter

melted butter for frying the crêpes
    and the oranges

2 oranges (preferably blood
    oranges)

2 Tbsp sugar

1 oz shot (2 Tbsp) Grand Marnier

½ cup orange juice (preferably
    freshly squeezed from blood
    oranges)

THIS RECIPE MASSACRES the traditional crêpes Suzette, but the result is a killer delicious dessert.

Combine the eggs, sugar, salt, milk, and water in a glass or ceramic bowl. Gradually whisk in the flour until thoroughly incorporated with no lumps. Whisk in the melted butter. Pour through a fine sieve into another glass or ceramic bowl, using a rubber spatula to push it through. Cover with plastic wrap and refrigerate at least 20 minutes or overnight.

The first crêpe that hits the pan is always a messy disaster, no matter how many times you've made these. You may have to adjust the heat and the consistency of the batter to get it right. Cut a few 8- to 10-inch squares of parchment paper for stacking the crêpes and set aside.

Get a crêpe pan or any non-stick pan onto medium heat. When the pan is hot, use a pastry brush to paint on an even coat of melted butter. Hold the pan with 1 hand, with the other holding a ladle of batter. Pour the batter in the middle while slowly swirling the pan. When the batter is evenly distributed, return the pan to the heat and cook until the crêpe is firm and the underside edges are golden and crispy.

Now it's time to flip. You can attempt to do so without a spatula. Just remember that if you think about it too hard, you'll mess up. Just flip it like it ain't no thing or it will sense your fear and be a flop instead of a flip.

When the other side is done, move the crêpe to a plate and start making another one. If they are too dry, mix in a teaspoon of cold water to the batter. You should end up with around 12 to 14 crêpes depending on the size and how many got flopped. Stack the finished crêpes between pieces of parchment paper.

Peel your oranges and hack them to small pieces with a sharp and sinister knife. They will splatter when you hack them, but how often do you get to hack something with a knife? Hopefully not often . . .

Get your sugar, shot of Grand Marnier (don't pour it directly from the bottle), and orange juice, as well as a barbecue lighter or long kitchen match, ready to go. Get another frying pan on super-high heat, put in some melted butter, and immediately throw in the hacked-up oranges and sprinkle on the sugar. After they have cooked for a few minutes to soften and release some moisture, add the Grand Marnier and *flambé*: pull the pan away from the heat source, add the shot of booze, and return it to the heat source. Ignite the booze with the lighter or match. When the flames subside, add the orange juice, and bring to a boil.

Fold each crêpe in half twice so you get a quarter-circle wedge.

Place 4 folded crêpes into the pan on the orange mess to form a circle. Cook until warm, flip so the other side gets some juices, and for each person serve 2 crêpes in a shallow bowl with a good scoop of macerated orange pulp, making sure there's enough sauce left over in the pan for the next batch or batches. Continue with the rest of the crêpes.

SERVES 2 CRÊPES TO 4 BLOODLUSTING PSYCHOS WITH HOPEFULLY A FEW LEFTOVER CRÊPES.

food you eat with a

hand

Society dictates that we eat our food with utensils. It may be in good taste to do so, but the food won't taste as good.

Your fingers are covered in nerve endings, including bajillions of taste buds that are so specialized they can only detect the delicious. When you combine these finger taste buds with the taste buds in your mouth, you get a super-enhanced flavour sensation. Food will taste up to ten times better depending on how many fingers you use to feed yourself. That is, each digit multiplies the effects.

I suggest you use all ten fingers for the full flavour experience.

angels and devils on horseback

There is a fine and streaky line between good and evil. And that line is made of bacon.

On one side you have the angel on horseback, a righteous oyster wrapped in bacon, but then on the other side the devil on horseback, a sinfully delicious bacon-wrapped prune. Don't bother choosing sides. You can be the neutral party and enjoy both on buttered toast.

angels

12 oysters, freshly shucked
   or pre-shucked
6 slices bacon
6 slices bread
butter

PREHEAT THE OVEN to broil.

Use the dull side of your knife to smooth and flatten out each slice of bacon so it is longer and wider. Cut each slice of bacon in half crosswise. Tightly roll the oyster in the bacon and place the wrapped oyster seam side down—so it won't unravel—in a deep baking dish. Alternately, you could secure it with a toothpick.

Line them up in the dish with plenty of space between, and blap them in the oven until the bacon is crispy on top.

Cut the crusts off your bread, and toast it all up while the angels are getting ready.

Butter the bread and serve with 2 angels per slice.

MAKES 12 ANGELS.

devils

12 large prunes
2 cups water
10 cracked peppercorns
6 whole cloves
1 tsp cinnamon
pinch of nutmeg
6 slices bacon
6 slices bread
butter

PREHEAT THE OVEN to broil. In a small pot, combine the prunes, water, peppercorns, cloves, cinnamon, and nutmeg. Bring to a boil, remove from the heat, and let it steep for 20 minutes.

While the prunes steep, use the dull side of your knife to smooth and flatten out each slice of bacon so it is longer and wider. Cut each slice of bacon in half crosswise. Drain the prunes. Tightly roll a prune in the bacon, and place the wrapped prune seam side down—so it won't unravel—in a deep baking dish. Alternately, you could secure it with a toothpick.

Line them up in a deep baking dish with plenty of space between, and blap them in the oven until the bacon is crispy on top.

Cut the crusts off your bread, and toast it all up while the devils are getting ready.

Butter the bread and serve with 2 devils per slice.

MAKES 12 DEVILS.

el grande lucha batalla del boca
the great fight battle of the mouth

Luchadores settle the score on the floor, *por favor*.

They are the fierce and hardened Mexican wrestlers of the *lucha libre* who will flatten anyone on the mat. A corn tortilla is a little like a lucha wrestling mat: it's a flat open space where a variety of heavy hitters come to throw down. Here are four champions of the *grande lucha batalla del boca*—the "great fight battle of the mouth."

el taco de pescados suave verde malo magro
the lean, mean, green fish taco

The suave *pescados* taco is rock-solid flavour and can handle anything. Its flexibility makes it easy to roll with any occasion or situation, and there is no challenge it can't wrap itself around.

The fish taco may seem like a departure from other, bigger, meatier contenders, but this lean-mean-green fish taco packs a spicy and refreshing punch that other tacos just can't contend with.

1 lb halibut, grouper, or snapper
    fillets, cut into 4 longish pieces

Fish marinade

½ cup vegetable oil

zest and juice of 1 lime

1 oz shot (2 Tbsp) tequila

1 jalapeño, finely minced

2 cloves garlic, grated

To serve

eight 6-inch soft corn tortillas

1 cup sour cream

½ cup salsa verde

5 green onions, thinly sliced

8 oz queso fresco (or feta—see
    sidebar below)

small bunch fresh cilantro

4 lime wedges

IN A CONTAINER or small baking dish, combine all the ingredients for the marinade. Make sure the fish is thoroughly covered in marinade, cover, then refrigerate for 30 to 60 minutes, but no more or the fish will start cooking in the lime juice.

Get a frying pan on medium heat—or better yet, fire up the barbecue. Place the fish pieces in the hot pan or directly on the grill and just let them sit for a while. Don't fuss with the fish or it will fall apart. Just let them mellow and cook on 1 side for about 4 minutes. Flip it once the bottom is brown or nicely grill-marked and continue cooking for another 4 minutes or so. It is done when the fish is flaky but still moist.

Put a damp paper towel or cloth over the tortillas and pop them in the microwave to soften for 20 seconds. Place 2 tortillas on top of each other on each plate.

Pile all the goods on the top tortilla: plop a scoop of sour cream down, then lay the hot fish on that. Pile on the salsa verde, green onion, queso fresco, and fresh sprigs of cilantro. Garnish the plate with lime wedges.

Fold the tortilla to eat it, but hold it strategically over the second tortilla so that everything drips down to it for a second helping. The messier it is the better it will taste.

MAKES 4 FISH TACOS.

SALSA FRESCO FOR GRINGOS

You don't have to speak Spanish to make decent salsa. But whatever you do, don't get the stuff in a jar—the word salsa is related to salad, for the love of *Dios*.

All you need to do is chop up a small red onion, a few tomatoes (or green tomatillos for salsa verde), a little minced jalapeño, and some fresh cilantro. Toss it in a bowl with a glug of oil, a pinch of salt, and a grated clove of garlic. That's it, *gringo*.

QUESO, POR FAVOR

Queso fresco literally means "fresh cheese." It is bright white, and moist but crumbly. You should be able to find it where Mexican specialty products are sold, along with Mexican oregano, achiote, and dried ancho chili.

If you can't find the real deal, tag in with some finely crumbled goat's feta.

el fajita flamante
the flaming fajita

The fajita is a raging, red-hot inferno of crazy deliciousness. And for these flaming fajitas, if you don't have a barbecue, I wouldn't even bother with this recipe. You really want those fiery grill marks on the steak.

The time and dedication needed to prep this are a startling contrast to the flash and fury of the actual cooking time. The marinade must be given at least a few hours, the barbecue must be preheated completely, and the veggies must be sliced caringly.

But these go down in a mind-blowin', rip-roarin' blaze of glory, and it is worth all the effort.

1 lb skirt steak

Marinade
juice and zest of 1 lime
2 oz shot a(¼ cup) tequila
¼ cup olive oil
3 cloves garlic, grated
1 tsp vanilla extract
2 Tbsp brown sugar
1 Tbsp kosher or sea salt
2 tsp dried Mexican oregano
1 tsp chipotle powder
½ tsp ground achiote
½ tsp ground ancho chili
¼ tsp cinnamon

Veggies
1 red onion
1 red pepper
1 green pepper
1 yellow pepper
2 Tbsp corn oil
2 oz shot (¼ cup) tequila blanco

To serve
eight 6-inch soft corn tortillas
4 oz queso fresco (see sidebar page 151)
1 cup salsa fresco (see sidebar page 151)
1 cup sour cream
1 cup guacamole or chunks of avocado

COMBINE ALL THE marinade ingredients in a large container or baking dish. Score both sides of the meat with shallow knife cuts no more than ¼ inch deep. Toss the meat in the marinade to coat, cover the container or dish, and let the marinade work its magic in the fridge for at least 2 hours or preferably overnight. Take it out of the fridge to get to room temperature for 30 minutes before tossing it on the heat.

Fire up your barbecue to super-inferno-hot.

Slice the onion thinly, and the peppers into thin ¼-inch strips. Get a large frying pan (preferably cast iron) on medium heat, and heat the oil. Pile on all the onions and peppers. Let them cook down nice and slow for about an hour, or until they get soft and all tangled. Finish the peppers with the shot of tequila and cook out the boozy smell.

Now it's time to blast the meat on the barbecue. Haul it out of the marinade, pat it dry a bit, and just slap it on the hot grill. This meat will cook super-fast, but you have to be careful not to overcook flank steak, or it will get really tough and rubbery. Wait 2½ minutes to make the nice grill marks, then flip it over and finish with 2½ more minutes on the other side. Transfer it to a plate and just let it rest for 10 minutes before you cut it.

When it is time to cut, get a really sharp knife, and slice the meat thinly on the bias and against the grain.

When you're about ready to serve, wrap the tortillas in a damp paper towel or damp clean dish cloth and microwave for 30 seconds to soften.

Serve the veggies straight from the pan with the sliced meat piled on top. Fill up little bowls with queso fresco, salsa fresco, sour cream, and guacamole (or chunks of avocado).

Serve up the tortillas, and invite people to mix and match their own toppings, fold, and eat.

SERVES 4 HEAVY-DUTY LUCHADORES.

bam-bam burrito

spicy bean and cheese burrito

Often imitated, but never defeated. Those wham-bam, 60-second-slam-in-the-microwave burritos are no match for the original, the real deal, the bam-bam burrito.

We're talking about a bean and cheese assault. This kind of explosive power can only come from slow-cooked beans melded with smoky flavours.

1 Tbsp vegetable oil

1 white onion, chopped

1 sweet red pepper, diced

1 poblano pepper, diced

1 can (19 oz) pinto beans, drained and rinsed

1 cup tomato juice

2 Tbsp adobo paste

2 cloves garlic, crushed

2 tsp salt

To serve

4 large flour tortillas

2 cups grated cheddar cheese

drizzling of hot sauce

GET A MEDIUM-SIZED pot over medium heat, and sweat the onion in the oil until tender and translucent. Toss in the diced peppers, and continue cooking until most of the moisture has slowly evaporated and the goods are getting nicely browned.

Then add the beans, tomato juice, adobo paste, garlic, and salt. Stir it up really well and make sure the adobo paste is evenly distributed. No one likes adobo clumps.

Drop the temperature down low and let the whole gloppy mix stew and simmer for 1 hour.

If you reheat it the next day, it will be even better.

When ready to serve, soften the tortillas in the micro for 20 seconds. In the centre of the tortilla, pile on a big scoop of gloppy beans. Top it with grated cheddar and as much hot sauce as you can handle. Fold in the side flaps, and holding them in, fold up the bottom flap over the beans. Then go with this flap's momentum and continue rolling until you end up with a burrito.

Eat it with *cerveza* and have a napkin handy.

MAKES 4 BLASTASTIC BURRITOS.

A DAB OF ADOBO

Adobo paste is typically used as a marinade for meats and gets most of its flavour from chipotle (smoked jalapeños). With a vast supporting cast of chilies, nuts, and spices, adobo is similar to a mole sauce. You are going to have to pick some up at a specialty shop.

los pequeños hermanos del enchilada
the little enchilada brothers' shredded chicken enchiladas

The Enchiladas are a fearsome brotherhood of little identical duodecaplets who attack in a pack. Don't be fooled by their tiny stature—they can take down a group of full-grown men.

Unfortunately they must split their wrestling wages 12 ways, so they have to budget carefully and share a lot of things, including a tightly packed apartment.

Fortunately, their favourite meal is also very cost-effective for feeding a bunch of wild hungry little wrestlers.

1 Tbsp vegetable oil

6 chicken thighs, skin on, bone in

2 oz shot (¼ cup) tequila

2 quarts tomato juice

2 Tbsp mole paste

1 Tbsp brown sugar

hot sauce of your choice, to taste

To serve

twelve 6-inch soft corn tortillas

8 oz queso fresco (or feta—see sidebar page 151)

1 head iceberg lettuce

2 limes

HOLY MOLE

Mole is a crazy mix of nuts, spices, and flavours (including cocoa) cooked down to a thick paste. All you need to know about making it is that you can pick some up at a Mexican or specialty foods shop and it keeps for ages in the fridge.

GET A BIG pot on medium heat, heat the oil, and place your chicken thighs skin side down. When the skin starts to brown, flip the thighs over and pour in the tequila. Let the boozy smell cook off for a minute and then add the tomato juice, mole paste, and brown sugar. Bring it to a simmer. Adjust the seasoning and add hot sauce to taste.

Now turn down the heat to low, and go practise your Learn to Speak Spanish tapes for 2 hours while the chicken simmers.

After 2 hours, pull out the thighs and pop them in a large bowl. Turn up the heat on the sauce, and let it bubble away for half an hour, until it reduces by at least half. In the meantime, start shredding the chicken. Just pull it off the bone with a fork or hand and discard the bones. Use your hands to finish shredding the chicken and to pick out any bits of cartilage or remaining bone.

Spoon some of the sauce into the bowl with the chicken, but only enough to bind the meat together. Save the rest for layering.

Preheat the oven to 350°F.

Pour a layer of sauce into the bottom of a large baking dish that will fit 12 rolled-up enchiladas.

Wrap the tortillas in a damp paper towel or damp clean dish cloth and microwave for 30 seconds to soften. Plop a scoop of shredded chicken across the centre of the tortilla, and roll the tortilla so the ends are open and the seam overlaps nicely. Place the enchilada seam side down in the baking dish. Keep rolling enchiladas and laying them tightly against each other in the baking dish. Top with the remaining sauce, and blap it in the oven for 20 minutes.

Chop your iceberg lettuce into chunks, and slice your lime into wedges.

Serve 2 enchiladas per person with a chunk of iceberg, a wedge of lime, a nice sprinkling of queso fresco, and an ice-cold *cerveza*.

SERVES 4 *LUCHADORES* OR 12 LITTLE DUODECAPLETS.

roman orgy feast

All roads lead to the orgy.

Ancient Romans knew how to indulge. Sure, Roman history recalls a handful of outspoken citizens and their efforts at creating social change and advancing Roman civilization, but the rest of Rome was a bunch of crazed party animals. With little work being done by the upper class, they had plenty of time to focus on eating, drinking, and carousing.

You can't have an orgy on an empty stomach. So here is a dinner party plan to get the juices flowing, which should lead to the inevitable inevitability.

The *cena* (dinner) was a threesome of courses divided into *gustum*, *mensa prima*, and *mensa secunda*. *Gustum* was the gustatory equivalent of foreplay leading to the *mensa prima*, a climactic thrust of savoury satisfaction, finished off with a leisurely sweet cuddle-up, the sweet-talking *mensa secunda*.

The courses were often broken up with bouts of entertainment, including poetry reading, music, and exotic dancers.

Nine diners would all hunker down on a U-shaped padded bench called a *triclinium* where they would have a very close and intimate meal served on a central table. They all perched on their left elbows, leaving their right hands free to eat with and use for other more dexterous pursuits.

A team of slaves was on hand to serve, entertain, clean up, and safely return their intoxicated masters home. Not to mention helping with other more hands-on matters.

Just remember, what happens in Rome, stays in Rome.

gustum

Gustum was an assortment of small nibbles like cured olives, cheeses, small fish, and eggs. It was like foreplay, with plenty of variety to be had during these starting rounds.

Wine sweetened with honey was used to get the juices flowing and helped lubricate the conversation toward more titillating topics.

eggs devilled

These sweet and savoury devilled eggs are a delicious start to a meal. The classic Roman combination of pine nuts, anchovy, and honey will pleasantly surprise your modern palate. And the boost of vitamin E will ensure a long night of high-endurance entertainment.

12 eggs
1 cup pine nuts
2 Tbsp honey
2 Tbsp white wine vinegar
1 Tbsp celery seed
1 tsp anchovy paste
pepper

TO HARD-BOIL THE EGGS, place them in a single layer in a large pot. Cover with cold water so they are submerged by 1 inch.

Bring the water to a boil over high heat, and as soon as it boils reduce the heat to medium. From this point, cook the eggs for exactly 10 minutes. Then run them under cold water for 5 minutes to stop the cooking immediately and to ensure they are chilled through completely.

In a blender or a large mortar and pestle, combine the rest of the ingredients until they become a chunky paste.

Shell all the eggs, cut them in half, and remove the yolks. Add the yolks to the blender or mortar and pestle and combine until the mixture is thick and smooth. Pipe or spoon the yolk mixture back into the yolk holes.

Serve on a large platter.

MAKES 24 DEVILLED EGGS.

julius caesar salad

Veni, vidi, vora . . . I came, I saw, I ate!

The Caesar salad we know and love today has nothing to do with Gaius Julius Caesar, the people's dictator. But with just a few tweaks that hearken back to ancient Rome, we can imagine that Gaius Julius Caesar would have enjoyed this salad.

½ cup olive oil

¼ cup blanched almonds

2 Tbsp white wine vinegar

1 Tbsp honey

4 anchovy fillets

4 cloves garlic

½ tsp celery seed

a crack of pepper

10 oz baby romaine lettuce, washed
   and dried

IN A BLENDER or mortar and pestle, combine all the ingredients except the romaine lettuce, and pulverize into a paste. The sauce will emulsify from the almonds and all the high-speed blending or mortar-and-pestle action. Note that this salad dressing tastes even better the next day, when the flavours have had a chance to settle down and mellow out.

Place the romaine in a large bowl and drizzle in the dressing. Toss to coat, and serve immediately in a large communal bowl. Do as the Romans do, and encourage your guests, from their reclined position on the couch, not to be shy about getting their fingers in there. Tell them to think of it as warming up their fingers.

Bring around a couple little bowls with warm water and a lemon wedge for a refreshing finger bath.

SERVES 6 LOYAL SERVANTS.

mensa prima

The main event is a barrage of multiple courses building up to a climax. An assortment of whole fish, stewed meats, and roasted birds comes out in rapid succession one after another, constantly pounding away like a wild, sweaty torrent of meat. It would be hard to maintain your decorum or to engage a fellow guest in conversation with the thrust of food coming at you from all directions.

roman chicken

The variety of birds they had in Rome would've made you weak at the knees. You could get any in any style you liked, from sweet to savoury. There were flocks from all over the known world, including goose, peacock, even flamingo. Sure, chicken to us can be a little mundane, but the Romans would have embraced it as they embraced all of the many birds available to them and revelled in natural selection.

Marinade

1 cup red wine

½ cup fish sauce

¼ cup honey

2 Tbsp ground cumin

1 Tbsp ground coriander

1 Tbsp dried oregano

2 tsp celery seed

1 tsp ground peppercorns

6 cloves garlic, minced

Chicken

12 chicken thighs

2 cups red grapes

1 cup kalamata olives, pitted

2 zucchini, in 1-inch chunks

1 red onion, in 1-inch chunks

1 cup pine nuts, toasted

PREHEAT THE OVEN to 425°F.

Combine the marinade ingredients in a dish that will fit the chicken thighs, and submerge the thighs while you prepare the other ingredients.

Place the grapes, olives, zucchini, and red onion into a large baking dish to form a roasting bed. Blap it in the oven for 30 minutes. Flip once while roasting.

After the 30 minutes are up, remove the chicken from the marinade and place it on top of the roasting bed. (Set aside the marinade for the sauce.) Leave some space between your thighs—it's nice to have some breathing room between your thighs. Roast the chicken for 20 to 25 minutes, until the top is crispy and the chicken is cooked through.

Pour the remaining marinade into a medium-sized pot and boil on high heat for about 30 minutes, until it reduces and gets syrupy.

When the chicken is done, remove it from the oven and drizzle on the sauce right in the baking dish, then let the whole thing rest for 10 minutes before serving.

Serve on a large platter, topped with the pine nuts. Eat with your fingers or with someone else's fingers.

SERVES 6 HUNGRY LEGIONAIRES.

lamb and celeriac stew

Lamb is young, tender, and extremely flexible. It was a favourite meat with the Romans, and it remains so with us because it works well roasted with sauce, or in heady rich stews like this recipe. This combines the classic lamb-and-anchovies with leeks and celery to make an awesome savoury stew. The anchovies are included to round out the flavours and to make the stew taste delicious. It's really subtle and won't end up making the whole thing taste fishy.

1 lamb shoulder, boned and tied

1 bottle white wine

12 anchovy fillets

6 cloves garlic

¼ cup whole cumin seeds

1 Tbsp celery seed

1 large celeriac, peeled and cut into
    1-inch cubes

olive oil

3 leeks, cleaned and sliced

6 ribs of celery, thinly sliced on the
    diagonal

¼ cup honey

1 Tbsp anchovy paste

salt and pepper

PLACE THE LAMB shoulder in a large pot. Add the white wine and enough water to cover it completely. Toss in the anchovy fillets, garlic cloves, cumin, and celery seed. Bring to a simmer over medium heat. Reduce heat to low and gently poach the lamb for 1 1/2 hours, or until it reaches an internal temperature of 155°F.

Transfer the lamb to a bowl and let it rest for 30 minutes. Crank the heat to high and boil the poaching liquid until it reduces to about 3 cups.

Dice the lamb into 1-inch cubes and set aside.

Strain the reduced poaching liquid through a sieve into a medium-sized pot, and put it over medium heat. Add the celeriac to get started on cooking it. Wipe the large pot clean and get it back over medium heat, get out some olive oil, and sweat the leeks and celery until soft. Add the celeriac along with the cooking liquid. Add the honey and anchovy paste, and simmer until the celeriac is tender. Adjust the seasoning with salt and pepper. Add the lamb back in and cook for 10 more minutes to heat it through.

Serve in bowls with spoons and flatbread. It's even better-tasting the next day—for breakfast, as the Romans do.

SERVES 6 RAVENOUS GLADIATORS.

mensa secunda

After the onslaught of meat you may be wondering
how a toga can feel so restrictive. You may have an
unbearable urge to disrobe or perhaps make a quick trip
to the vomitorium to help relieve some pressure. And
then you can settle things down a bit with something
delightfully sweet—a sweet cap to the gut-busting eat-
stravaganza.

It is a nice opportunity to slow down the pace and
recharge while you sweet-talk the others into extending
the party with a *commissatio.*

"the great" dates

It goes without saying that Alexander the Great was a great guy. He could get all the dates he wanted, and this sweet and spicy dish is named after him. These dates are so sweetly potent that they will give you enough energy to take over the world . . . or at least the known world.

½ cup honey

3 Tbsp cold butter

40 whole almonds

1 Tbsp cinnamon

20 Medjool dates, pitted

pinch of salt

PREHEAT THE OVEN to broil.

In a small saucepan, stir the honey and butter over medium heat. When the honey butter is rich and syrupy, throw in the almonds and toss to coat. Remove the coated almonds with a slotted spoon onto a plate, and sprinkle with the cinnamon. Set aside the honey syrup.

When the almonds are cool enough to handle, place 2 almonds into each date where the pit used to be. Line the stuffed dates in a baking dish in legionary formation, and drizzle on the remaining honey syrup. Broil for 10 minutes so they get nice and tasty-roasted.

Let them cool slightly before serving with wine.

SERVES 10 GUESTS (2 DATES EACH).

roman crêpes
with sweet stewed raisins and ricotta

The Romans had limitless appetites and imaginations, never stopping short of indecent when it came to satisfying their senses. This was true for sweets. Lurid, exotic, and spicy combinations might almost be too scintillating for our modern sensibilities, but of course we and the Romans do not share the same taboos.

Stewed raisins

1 cup white wine

2 Tbsp honey

1 Tbsp ground cumin

1 tsp ground coriander

pinch of salt

1 cup golden raisins

Crêpes

3 eggs

2 cups milk

½ cup cold water

pinch of salt

2 cups whole wheat or spelt flour

Et cetera

¼ cup melted butter

8 oz ricotta (see page 39 for homemade ricotta)

½ cup toasted crushed hazelnuts

COMBINE THE WINE, honey, spices, and salt in a small pot. Bring to a boil on high, and reduce the liquid by half. Place the raisins in a small bowl and pour the hot liquid over them. Cover with a plate and allow it to steep and cool to room temperature. Then chill it in the fridge.

Combine the eggs, milk, cold water, and salt. Slowly whisk in the flour a bit at a time to make a smooth batter. Let the batter rest in the fridge for at least 1 hour or preferably overnight.

For the crêpes, cut a few 8- to 10-inch squares of parchment paper and set aside. Heat an 8-inch crêpe pan (or non-stick frying pan) over medium heat. Add some melted butter, and evenly ladle on some crêpe batter while tilting and rotating the pan to evenly distribute the batter. Cook until the crêpe is firm and the underside edges are crispy and golden. Flip the crêpe and finish cooking. Pile the finished crêpes on a plate with parchment paper between them.

For each crêpe, spoon a bit of ricotta in a row along the middle, and add a scoop of raisins. Tightly roll into a cylinder.

Serve 2 crêpes per guest, drizzled with some of the liquid from the stewed raisins and with a few crushed hazelnuts scattered on top.

WILL MAKE ABOUT 14 CRÊPES, DEPENDING ON HOW BIG YOU MAKE THEM AND HOW MANY GET MESSED UP.

commissatio

If you are still awake after
the waves of wine, eating, and
heavy petting, you can do one of
two things. First choice is to pass out
and let your slaves haul your sloppy self
home. Second is to go for a quick visit (again!)
to the vomitorium, drink through the slump,
and entice others to join you as you indulge in other
sensory stimulation.

Even in Rome everyone knows that after the party
comes the afterparty. The *commissatio* was a free-for-all,
open-bar drinking fest that went on and on to the break
of dawn.

welcome to the academy for incendiary arts

Greetings, and welcome to the Academy for Incendiary Arts, where all you fire-breathing dragons will be working through three degrees in the incendiary culinary arts to complete your BFA (or Bachelor of Fire Arts). This innovative program will teach you the techniques needed to succeed as a fire-breathing chef. Each level builds on the techniques from the previous one, helping to ignite your passion for cooking with direct flame.

Being able to breathe fire is not a prerequisite, and all non-fire-breathers will be provided with a heavy-duty blowtorch to complete the assignments and practical examinations.

Register now for classes, and get on the fast track to your career in this exciting field.

first degree in the bachelor of fire arts
indoors s'mores

Your first lesson is a great opportunity to get to know your flame-throwing capabilities with something that you are probably familiar with . . . s'mores.

Traditionally, marshmallows are cooked on an open fire, but with this recipe you must work with focused and controlled heat from a direct flame. This way, you will learn all about precision cooking and hopefully inflame an inner passion for it. Your mastery of marshmallow accuracy will bolster the confidence you need to move onto the next degree of the Fire Arts program.

6+ large marshmallows
1 milk chocolate bar, in 6 chunks
12 graham crackers

THE TRICK IS to get the marshmallows as evenly brown as possible while ensuring the insides get enough heat to start melting.

Fix 1 marshmallow at the end of a long metal fork or skewer. Hold this with 1 hand, and hold the blowtorch with the other. Move the marshmallow to various parts of the flame to figure out where the hottest part of the flame is. You may be surprised to find it's a couple inches from the mouth of the flame thrower, not the bulk of the flame itself. You want to move the marshmallow to just around the hot point, using a feathery touch.

You may need to move both hands to get the spot right on. Slowly twirl the fork or skewer so that the rest of the marshmallow gets exposed to the flame. Your goal is to give the marshmallow an even brown colour.

You will be experiencing some trial and error. Before long you will probably light one on fire, but don't let that discourage you. Just blow it out and try again with another marshmallow. If it's about to do it again, blow on it gently to inhibit a wildfire from spreading all over your marshmallow.

When you've honed your skills and you get a hot gooey marshmallow, stick it between 2 graham crackers with a chunk of chocolate, and get the sticky mess into your mouth in as few bites as possible. Repeat with the remaining marshmellows, graham crackers, and chocolate.

MAKES 6 S'MORES.

INTRODUCTION TO SAFETY

At the Academy for Incendiary Arts we pride ourselves on safety. Although most of our students are equipped with thick fire-retardant scales, some of our softer-fleshed students are at risk for serious danger from burns and explosions. Here are some safety tips to help you stay on the job and out of the hospital.

1. Use a heavy-duty blowtorch from the hardware store, not the itsy-bitsy ones from the craft store or kitchen store.
2. Carefully read the safety instructions that come with the blowtorch.
3. Get your hair out of the way and do not wear baggy clothes. Both can get in the line of fire.
4. If you are not using a self-igniting blowtorch, ignite using a blowtorch spark starter.
5. Never leave the blowtorch near a heat source like your stove. Also, the counter you are working on should be far from a heat source.
6. Be super-aware of where you are pointing the flame at all times.
7. What you plan to torch should always be in a flameproof container like ceramic or metal. Not wood, glass, or plastic.

second degree in the bachelor of fire arts
crème brûlée

Now that you have learned the basics, it is time for something more to test your precision and discipline and to hone your skills. You must challenge yourself with a variety of crème brûlée applications.

In spite of the burning implied by the term *brûlée*, the sugar is not burnt black, but rather melted to form a dark golden pane of glass above the velvety custard below.

After this you will be ready for the final level of the Academy.

For the custard

4 eggs (you'll be using only the
    yolks)

¼ cup sugar, divided

1 cup 2% milk

½ cup heavy cream

1 vanilla pod, slit open (do not use
    vanilla extract)

For brûléeing

1 tsp demerara sugar

1 tsp brown sugar

1 tsp cane sugar

1 tsp granulated sugar

OH SH— UGAR!

Keep careful track of each ramekin throughout the lesson so you can make a mental note about which sugar you prefer, not just to eat but to work with. Some will be great melters, while others may burn too quickly for you. The resulting sugar pane will also vary in its thickness and crunch factor. Experimenting like this will help you become a crème brûlée master.

PREHEAT THE OVEN to 325°F.

Separate the eggs with the yolks in a large bowl. (Keep the egg whites for an omelette or whatever you like.) Add half the sugar to the egg yolks and whisk vigorously until the colour of the yolks lightens a couple shades.

Set aside a spouted container with a sieve resting on top.

Get a pot on the stove with the milk, cream, rest of the sugar, and vanilla pod over medium heat, stirring frequently to ensure the sugar dissolves. The moment it boils, pull it off the heat and let it cool down for 5 minutes.

Pour half the milk mixture slowly into the egg yolks, whisking continuously. Pour the tempered yolk mixture back into the pan while whisking gently. Now pour everything through the sieve into the spouted container.

Place four 2 oz ceramic ramekins in a deep baking dish. Fill the ramekins evenly with the custard. Fill the baking dish with hot tap water so it comes halfway up the outside of the ramekins.

Gently blap the dish in the oven for 35 to 40 minutes. The custard will have a little wiggle when it is done.

Take the whole thing out of the oven. Carefully remove the ramekins and place on a plate, and chill in the fridge for 2 hours.

Get a chilled ramekin and dump the demerara sugar onto the top. Tilt and gently shake the ramekin until the sugar covers the entire surface. Dump out the excess sugar.

Fire up the blowtorch. Carefully hold the ramekin underneath by your fingertips, making sure your hand isn't in the line of fire. You want to hold the ramekin instead of leaving it on the counter so you can control where the flame hits.

Aim your flame at the sugar. Keep moving the ramekin with your hand. As soon as the sugar starts to bead up, redirect the flame to another spot. When the whole surface is beaded, go back and brûlée the whole surface again so it melts just a little more. Make sure you get the edges, and be careful not to let the sugar get too dark or burn.

Repeat this procedure with the rest, using the different sugars.

Re-chill and serve with a small fancy spoon to crack the hard sugar and to get to the soft custard inside.

MAKES 4 CRÈME BRÛLÉES WITH 4 DIFFERENT SUGAR PANES.

third degree in the bachelor of fire arts
crispy-skinned trout sandwich
with charred green onion and jalapeño dressing on a toasted baguette with feta and red pepper!

Now that you are comfortable with direct-flame cooking, it is time to create a complex main dish using the techniques you've learned so far with new ingredients. With your increasing manual dexterity and understanding of temperature control you will be able to tackle more and more complicated tasks.

This third degree rounds out your program, and after becoming a graduate you will have the confidence to succeed in the real world of incendiary cooking.

1 medium red pepper

1 jalapeño

4 green onions

1 clove garlic

2 Tbsp rice vinegar

big pinch of salt

¼ cup olive oil

1 crusty baguette

2 small river trout fillets, skin on,
    bones removed

vegetable oil for preparing the trout
    for torching

arugula

2 oz feta, crumbled

FIRE UP YOUR blowtorch and start with your red pepper. Jab it securely onto the end of a fork and scorch the living daylights out of it. You cannot burn it too much—get it black as a piece of charcoal. While it's still hot, put it in an airtight container and put on the lid. The steaming will make peeling off the skin easier.

The same applies to the jalapeño. Jab it with a fork and char it so badly that you need to check dental records to find out it was a jalapeño. Set it aside to cool. (It doesn't need to go into a container.)

Hold the green onions using a pair of metal tongs, and go over the green parts with the hot part of the flame until they start to turn black, but don't char them as badly as the peppers. Spend some extra time on the white parts. Let them cool, then cut into 2-inch lengths.

In the sink under cool running water, rinse both peppers, using your thumbs to rub away the charred black surface. They should both be soft enough to be pulled open so you can scoop out the seeds and stem by hand. Slice the red pepper into strips and set aside.

Place the jalapeño, green onions, garlic, vinegar, salt, and oil in a food processor, and blend until smooth.

Split your baguette lengthwise in 2, and give it a nice gentle toasting with your blowtorch. Slather as much of the green dressing as you like on both sides of the bread before you move on to cooking the trout.

Make sure the trout does not have any remaining bones. Tweezers are the best way to remove them. Rub both sides with a little bit of oil, and lay them skin side down on an inverted metal baking tray. Don't do this blowtorching on a plate or even a ceramic plate—it will shatter into a bajillion pieces.

Work your way up and down the trout to give it an even gentle heat. Do this slowly and evenly until the flesh starts to get little dark flecks, and the trout is cooked most of the way through.

Pick up the trout and lay it cooked side down on the bread. Go over the skin carefully with the blowtorch until the skin is lovely and crispy. Top with little red pepper strips, arugula, and a good sprinkling of feta cheese.

Congratulations! You are now a proud graduate of the Academy for Incendiary Arts.

MAKES 1 LONG SANDWICH.

mega kaiju burger battel royale

There's Kaiju Big Battel, but then there's *Mega Kaiju Burger Battel Royale*.

Super-mega-beefy monster contenders enhanced with giga-super-duper-powers are waging a neverending battle for burger supremacy.

Whether it is a greasy slop-burger, a mutant meatosauruswich, or some mad-genius chef's attempt to make the most expensive burger, they all think they have what it takes to be the best burger . . . but only *one* can truly be the best burger.

captain boigah

If you think you can beat the *boigah*, then step up, the captain is taking all challengers.

Back before burgers were soiled with guacamole or peanut sauce, there was the original *boigah*. A chunk of flame-grilled ground beef with a modest assortment of toppings on a sesame bun. Why is this simple combination not respected enough in this world, this world that is constantly trying to change and "improve" it?

The reigning champ is and should always be the Captain Boigah.

1 ¼ lb grass-fed ground beef

vegetable oil to grease the grill

2 nice tomatoes

8 leaves of lettuce

1 red onion

2 dill pickles

4 sesame-seed buns

salt and pepper

yellow mustard, as needed

ketchup, as needed

mayonnaise, as needed

CAPTAIN OBVIOUS

If this seems like such an obvious recipe to you, then why is your mouth watering?

Consider it a reminder that you haven't had a good burger in a very long time. Those floppy sad sacks of a meal you get from fast-food joints are not burgers, they aren't even food. They are a sorry, pathetic excuse for what a burger should be. When you see things get that processed, it helps to go back to when things were good.

PREHEAT THE BARBECUE to high.

Divide the beef into 4 equal chunks. Don't muck around, just roll each chunk around until it makes a ball. Flatten the balls into burger patties that are larger than the bun. Get 'em back in the fridge while you get all the other stuff ready.

Prepare everything as if you were making the last burger you'll ever eat. Lovingly cut the tomatoes into thick slices with a sharp knife so they don't squish, gently rinse the lettuce and pat it dry, expertly slice the red onion into very thin slices like you're a deli slicer, and carefully carve the pickles into thick planks.

Gently cradle the buns while you cut them in half evenly, trying not to knock off any of the golden-sesame flavour capsules.

Lay the burger patties on the red-hot grill, and don't touch them at all until you see blood bead up on top. Gingerly flip the burgers over. Let them finish cooking without messing around with them. Forget about the nonsense about making criss-cross grill marks.

Transfer the patties onto a plate. Thoughtfully sprinkle the patties with salt and pepper.

Now—as if you were Michelangelo carving the David—create the burger. Starting with the bottom of the bun, dazzle on some yellow mustard and ketchup. Transfer the beef into the cradle of the bun like it was your first-born. With great providence pile on the onion, pickles, lettuce, and tomato. Give the top half of the bun a generous slathering of mayonnaise, and top the burger with the golden sesame crown.

Enjoy with a bottled beer and nothing else.

SERVES 4 NOSTALGIC BURGERVORES.

the bastard child of mr. croque

He is a *monsieur* among sandwiches . . . and let's just say he gets around town.

Croque Monsieur ("Mister Crunchy") is a name spoken fondly of in bars and cafés throughout France. However, because he is so famous, numerous bastards have been spawned.

This recipe is one such bastardization of the French classic.

FRENCH BASTARDS

As the bastard child of a Frenchman, I'm thankful that the apple falls far, far away from the tree. Just like me, this recipe is a drastic takeoff from the original.

The only thing this sandwich got from the original is a name and a few physical resemblances—but this bastard is much better, if I do say so myself.

4 eggs

2 Tbsp heavy cream

4 thick slices of French bread
(from a loaf, not a baguette)

4 Tbsp butter, divided

½ lb really good ham

8 oz Gruyère or Emmenthal, grated

a gloop of Dijon mustard

some gherkin pickles

PREHEAT THE OVEN to broil and set the rack in the middle.

Break the eggs in a shallow bowl, add the cream, and beat with a whisk.

Get an ovenproof frying pan (all metal, no plastic) on the stove on medium heat.

Dip the French bread in the egg mixture and coat both sides. Really get it soaked, even mushing it a bit so it sucks up all the egg mixture. Once the pan is hot, drop in half the butter, and when it is foaming place 2 pieces of the egg-soaked bread in the pan.

When the bottom edges get golden brown, you can flip the bread.

Immediately pile half the ham onto each of the 2 slices, then top that with half the cheese, and quickly get the pan into the oven.

The heat from the pan will cook the bottom, while the broiler will make the cheese so unbelievably crispy and crunchy that you will forget about all the other ham and cheese sandwiches that you have ever encountered in the past.

When the top is golden, get the sandwiches out of the oven, out of the pan, and onto serving plates with some Dijon mustard and gherkins. Repeat with the remaining 2 pieces of bread.

FEEDS 4 LUCKY BASTARDS.

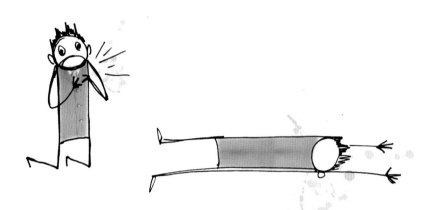

enjoy every sandwich, it could be your last

There are many ways to die, and some are more appealing than others . . . drifting off to sleep and being constricted between a great pair of legs are near the top of my list. But the top one on the list is to die in the throes of gastronomic ecstasy.

There are a few options available: *fugu*, the Japanese fish-roulette, whose liver, ovaries, and skin are highly poisonous; an assortment of mushrooms from the wild potentially sending you on a psychedelic trip to the next world; or finally, with ingredients more easily accessible, the Heart Attack Sandwich, which could probably take down a triathlete with a single bite.

Just because you are not dead doesn't mean you are truly living.

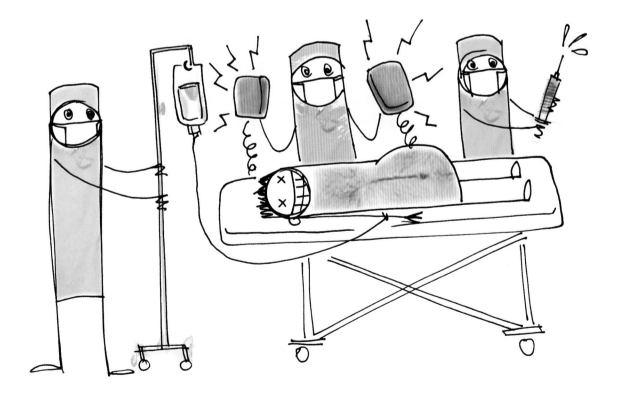

heart attack sandwich

6 slices thick-cut bacon

3 eggs

4 thick slices of gleaming white fibreless bread

three 1 oz slabs of cheddar cheese

3 Tbsp mayonnaise

potato chips

IN A LARGE frying pan, cook the bacon until crispy. Place the bacon directly onto a plate, and not on paper towels—we want all the excess grease.

Now, the bacon has left behind a pan full of bacon drippings. Fry the eggs in it, cooking the yolks hard to keep them from spilling out in the sandwich later. Transfer the eggs to the same plate as the bacon.

Layer the sandwich like so . . . bread, cheese, egg, bacon, mayonnaise, potato chips, bread . . . and so on, until you have 3 layers of filling smooshed between 4 pieces of bread. Using what is left of the bacon fat, fry the sandwich until it is golden brown on both sides.

MAKES 1 MEMORABLE LAST MEAL.

NON-SURGEON GENERAL'S WARNING

If I were the Surgeon General, I would probably tell you never to eat this sandwich. But I'm not the Surgeon General, so I can tell you I think it is something worth trying at least once . . . even if it is the last thing you do. But of course I'd never suggest a sandwich-assisted suicide.

metric conversions

VOLUME

¼ tsp	1 mL
½ tsp	2 mL
1 tsp	5 mL
2 tsp	10 mL
1 Tbsp	15 mL
2 Tbsp	30 mL
3 Tbsp	45 mL
¼ cup	60 mL
5 Tbsp	75 mL
⅓ cup	80 mL
½ cup	125 mL
⅔ cup	160 mL
¾ cup	185 mL
1 cup	250 mL
1 ¼ cups	310 mL
1 ½ cups	375 mL
2 cups	500 mL
3 cups	750 mL
4 cups	1 L
6 cups	1.5 L
8 cups	2 L
1 pint	500 mL
1 quart	1 L
1 oz shot	30 mL
2 oz shot	60 mL
2 oz ramekins	60 mL

WEIGHT

1 oz	30 g
2 oz	60 g
3 oz	90 g
4 oz	125 g
6 oz	175 g
8 oz	250 g
½ lb	250 g
10 oz	300 g
1 lb	500 g
1 ¼ lb	625 g
1 ½ lb	750 g
2 lb	1 kg

LENGTH

⅛ inch	3 mm
¼ inch	6 mm
½ inch	1 cm
1 inch	2.5 cm
2 inches	5 cm
3 inches	8 cm
4 inches	10 cm
5 inches	12 cm
6 inches	15 cm
7 inches	18 cm
8 inches	20 cm
10 inches	25 cm
11 inches	28 cm
12 inches	30 cm

TEMPERATURE

155°F	68°C
190°F	88°C
200°F	95°C
250°F	120°C
300°F	150°C
325°F	160°C
350°F	180°C
375°F	190°C
400°F	200°C
425°F	220°C
450°F	230°C
475°F	240°C
500°F	260°C

CAN SIZES

14 oz	398 mL
19 oz	540 mL

index